8992 Bennett, Roger,
     1970-

And you shall know us
by the trail of our
vinyl.

$24.95

And You Shall Know Us by the Trail of Our Vinyl

SHAINDELE

SINGS

THE
SONGS
OF HER
PEOPLE

ORCHESTRA & CHORUS
Conducted By ABRAHAM ELLSTEIN

MARGOT
RECORDS

M 613

LP 101
EL-AL
33⅓ LONG PLAYING

YOUR
SEDER

AN AMERICAN HOME SERVICE FOR THE PASSOVER

conducted by
Rabbi Robert I. Kahn, DHL.

This Seder Service follows the UNION HAGGADAH.
Copyright permission to contents of the 'Haggadah'
granted by Central Conference of American Rabbis.

LONDON
INTERNATIONAL
TW 91660

טופול
בשירי
מלחמה

WAR SONGS
TOPO

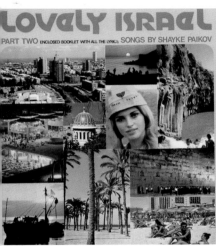

And You Shall Know Us by the Trail of Our Vinyl

The Jewish Past as Told by the Records We Have Loved and Lost

Roger Bennett and Josh Kun

Crown Publishers
New York

Crown Publishers/New York

Copyright © 2008 by In Loving Memory of the Recent Past and Josh Kun

Cataloging-in-Publication Data is available from the Library of Congress.

ISBN 978-0-307-39467-5

Printed in Malaysia

Design by Kay Schuckhart/Blond on Pond

10   9   8   7   6   5   4   3   2   1

First Edition

Roger Bennett: To my grandfather Samuel; my two gents, Samson and Ber; and my daughter, Zion

Josh Kun: For Mort and Joni Kamins, Nicholas and Bertha Kun

C O N T E N T S

FOREWORD BY NEIL SEDAKA 8

INTRODUCTION 10

What It Sounds Like: Ann Powers on Barbra Streisand's "Lullaby for Myself" from *Streisand Superman*

1. MEN'S WEARHOUSE: THE CHANGING SARTORIAL STYLES OF THE GREAT CANTORS 26

What It Sounds Like: Josh Rosenfeld on "Entebbe" by the Miami Boys Choir from *Miami Choir Boys*

Spotlight On: Sol Zim—The Original Star of David

2. THE YIDDISH ARE COMING: HOW VINYL KEPT A DYING LANGUAGE ALIVE 44

What It Sounds Like: Michael Wex on Marty Gale's *Sexy Stories with a Yiddisha Flavor*

Spotlight On: At Home and Abroad with the Barry Sisters

3. GO DOWN MOSES: THE MUSIC OF BLACK-JEWISH RELATIONS 62

What It Sounds Like: Lamont Dozier on the Temptations' "Fiddler on the Roof Medley" from *On Broadway*

What It Sounds Like: Oliver Wang on David Axelrod's *The Auction*

4. WHO NEEDS A SYNAGOGUE WHEN YOU HAVE A RECORD PLAYER IN YOUR LIVING ROOM?: THE JEWISH HOLIDAYS AS LONG-PLAYING RECORDS 78

5. ME LLAMO STEINBERG: THE JEWISH LATIN CRAZE 94

What It Sounds Like: Wil-Dog Abers of Ozomatli on Juan Calle and His Latin Lanzmen's *Mazel Tov, Mis Amigos*

6. LAUGHING AT 33 RPM: THE VINYL WORLD OF COMEDY   112

What It Sounds Like: Sandra Bernhard on Pearl Williams's *Bagels and Lox*

What It Sounds Like: Aimee Bender on Sophie Tucker's *Bigger and Better Than Ever*

7. "OH WHAT A NIGHT!": PARTIES, WEDDINGS, LOVE, AND GOOD OLD-FASHIONED HAPPINESS   134

Spotlight On: America on the Roof

8. THE SOUND OF SUFFERING: HOLOCAUST, SOVIET JEWRY, AND MARTYRDOM ON VINYL   146

What It Sounds Like: Etgar Keret on "Pharaoh, Let My People Go" by Theodore Bikel, from *Silent No More*

9. HAIFA IN HI-FI: THE EVER-EVOLVING NOTION OF ISRAEL   158

Spotlight On: Gadi Elon—A Lover, Not a Fighter

10. STOP SINGING OUR SONGS: NON-JEWISH MASTERS OF THE JEWISH MELODY   198

What It Sounds Like: Norman Lear on Jon Yune's *Ose Shalom*

11. THE FOLK EXPLOSION: THE LAST DAYS OF JEWISH VINYL   206

What It Sounds Like: Shalom Auslander on Abi and Esther Ofarim's "Cinderella Rockefella" from *Cinderella Rockefella*

Spotlight On: The House That Theo Built

CONCLUSION   226

AFTERWORD BY MAIRA KALMAN   229

CONTRIBUTOR BIOS   232

BIBLIOGRAPHY   234

ACKNOWLEDGMENTS   236

FOREWORD

By Neil Sedaka

I was raised on Yiddish music. Growing up in Brighton Beach, Brooklyn, after World War II, I thought the whole world was Jewish. My mother would play the Barry Sisters' records, and we would listen to *The Sunday Morning Simcha* on the radio.

My mother was of Polish/Russian Ashkenzic descent. My father's parents came from Istanbul, Turkey; Sephardic Jews. My grandmother, Norna, played Ladino records in the house. As a three-year-old, the sound of them frightened me. So I would lock myself in the bathroom. I would hear the (Ashkenazy) songs at bar mitzvahs, family gatherings, and picnics where Uncle Joey, Aunt Frieda, and Aunt Minnie would sing "Bei Mir Bist Du Schoen" in perfect three-part harmony. Also, at the Brighton Beach Baths, there were acts who played accordion and fiddle, such as Harold Stern and Jeannie Clair.

As I began listening to more music, while studying at the Juilliard School of Music as a piano student, I made an interesting discovery.

The R&B black blues songs had a distinct similarity in feeling to the Jewish songs. I think because we were both oppressed and had to deal with being second-class citizens, it came out in the music we wrote. Listen to George Gershwin's *Porgy and Bess*, the magnificent minor tune of "Summertime." Or B. B. King's "The Thrill Is Gone." You can hear the suffering and pathos in them. You can hear the Chaplin-esque quality—melancholy and hope at the same time.

When I was a musician in the Catskills at my future mother-in-law's hotel, The Esther Manor, I started to play "Vi Ahin Zol Ich Geyn," "Eishes Chayil," "Mein Shtetele Belz," and "Schoen Vi Di L'Vone." They were always crowd pleasers in the late '50s and early '60s.

Years later I decided to record a CD: *Brighton Beach Memories—Sedaka Sings Yiddish*. To my amazement, it went to the top ten on Amazon.com. It proved to me that there are many young Jewish families trying to preserve this wonderful culture, language, and

Neil Sedaka with the Tokens
Untitled
Vernon Records, 1960

music. I can even hear the Yiddish influences in some of my early compositions: "You Mean Everything to Me," "One More Ride on the Merry-Go-Round," and "The Big Parade."

There is such emotional power in this music. A Canadian woman sent me a letter and told me how she visits her mother regularly in an old-age Jewish home. She told me when she plays my CD, the elderly people with dementia and Alzheimer's start dancing and singing along to the music, shocking their friends and family. Isn't it wonderful how music is so therapeutic? It makes me cry tears of joy.

When I look through these albums, I'm reminded of just how beautiful and varied this legacy is. This is a rich heritage that we still don't know enough about.

This book is proof that this music does not just belong to the past. Seeing how Roger and Josh have hunted down all of these old LPs makes me hopeful for what the next generation will do with all of these powerful stories.

INTRODUCTION

"The miracle of collecting . . . is what you really collect is always yourself."
—Jean Baudrillard, *Le Système des Objets*

First, a confession is in order.

This book is, quite obviously, about album covers, and there are over four hundred of them on the pages that follow to prove it, but really it wouldn't exist if it weren't for two old black-and-white family photographs that have haunted us for years. The photographs are from generations past, and neither of us knows much about them. One is a portrait of a dashing, tender-faced great-grandfather in Hungarian military garb, about to share a fancy meal with his fellow soldiers. The other is a shot of a more menacing great-great-grandfather reputed to be a mob boss in pre-war Poland. Their names have been lost, the facts of their lives barely known.

The two of us came of age in two different places—Los Angeles, California, and Liverpool, England—but we both inherited family histories that were blurred. For one of us, growing up in Liverpool was about Polish butchers becoming kosher meat emperors, about a great-grandfather who built one of Liverpool's biggest shuls but had great-grandsons who avoided going to synagogue at all costs, and about elders who spoke Yiddish and studied Talmud but whose sons and daughters wouldn't know a Talmud if it landed on their heads. For the other, Los Angeles was where modern Orthodox Hungarian immigrants, Holocaust survivors, and Reform Russian Jewish farmers reborn as clothiers with impressively low golf handicaps bumped into one another. There were Passover dinners and High Holy Day out-

Josh Kun's great-grandfather (first on lower left)

Roger Bennett's great-great-grandfather

Barry Manilow
Greatest Hits
Arista, 1975

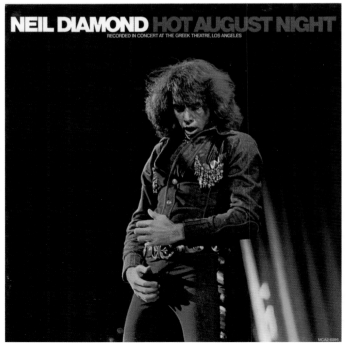

Neil Diamond
Hot August Night
MCA, 1972

ings, but there were also Easter egg hunts and catered Christmas Eve dinners.

Our parents were our mediators, our filters between worlds. Our sense of our Jewishness was based increasingly on assimilation, and with it came an ebbing sense of family history. Like all children, our parents had forged their lives to look different from that of their parents. They would carry some things on and bury others. They were closer to the past than we were and could touch it and hide it in a single stroke. As their sons, we eventually realized that what we'd inherited was somehow incomplete. Who were these men in these photos? Why could no one tell us how they lived and what they believed in? We both became living examples of that old anthropological saw: What the son wishes to forget, the grandson wishes to remember.

Our individual desire to remember soon began to color the other thing we had in common, an intense love of music. The dominant force in our teenage years, music was our religion. Bands like Adam & the Ants, the Human League, and a Flock of Seagulls were our priests. Live Aid was the zenith, an event that reinforced our belief that music had something important to say and, as quickly as you could say Hands Across America, could solve all the world's problems. We went on to embrace everything the marketers threw at us—reggae, Latin music, hip-hop—everything, that is, except Jewish music. In our childhood homes, Jewish music meant pop icons of the 1970s and '80s like Barbra Streisand, Neil Diamond, and Barry Manilow, and maybe a version of "Hava Nagila" or "Tzena, Tzena, Tzena" sung by the Weavers thrown in for good measure.

As we were growing up, there seemed to be only two kinds of music made by Jews. On the one hand, there was Barbra singing "People" or Barry belting "Mandy" or Neil rocking through "Sweet Caroline," that holy triumvirate of Brooklyn-born Jews who managed to spin their roots into massive showbiz windfalls—Jewish enough to fill their people with pride but not so Jewish that they couldn't fill stadiums full of Irish Catholics who know every word to "I Write the Songs." We knew they were Jews, but more important, we knew they were American icons. To paraphrase Manilow, it looked like they had made it, and made it big—so big that each of them had released not one but two Christmas albums.

Streisand got her big break playing Fanny Brice and went on to do yeshiva-boy drag as Yentl, but she still managed to rule soft rock radio with LPs like *Streisand Superman* and *Guilty*, her glorious collaboration with the Bee Gees' Barry Gibb. Manilow's lush disco soap opera "Copacabana" may have been the theme song at pretty much every bar mitzvah we went to, but it also made every Jewish teenager in America secretly want to catch the next plane to Havana and be glamorously Cuban like Rico and Lola. And with Diamond's *Hot August Night*—especially with its unforgettable cover shot of Neil with his mouth agape, his furry chest bared, and his cocked arms summoning forth unseen carnal energies—we had our first real proof that little Jewish kids could grow up to be universally worshiped Rock Gods.

On the other hand, there was the music we were spoon-fed at Hebrew school, Jewish traditional songs and happy Hebrew folk tunes that sounded stale and desperate to be loved. Sure, some of them stayed with us (who doesn't like a good speed round of "Dayenu" now and again?), but they were presented to us as obligatory links to a frozen heritage that didn't seem to have anything to do with who we thought we were. As with our own family histories, we were being given shadowy pictures of our past. We wanted more. We wanted what wasn't there.

As we grew older and as our commitment to music grew more intense, we both began to learn that the "more" we sought could actually be found in the most unlikely place: not in Jewish museums, Jewish history books, or even family photo albums, but in the place we both trusted most—the record store. It was there, buried in the used-LP bins, that our missing history began to reveal itself. It was through thousands of twelve-inch long-playing records collecting dust in thrift stores that our family photographs started to speak to us.

All it took was one magnificent find—*Bagels and Bongos* by the Irving Fields Trio, an album originally released in 1959 with a flamboyant cocktail-hour cover and an elegantly mashed-up sound: "Hava Nagila" resounded as "Havana Nagila," and "Rabbi Eile Melech" reenergized as "Miami Merengue." The interpretation of Jewish songs set to Latin rhythms was familiar enough to connect with, yet its playful riffing, creativity, and irresistible listenability were sufficiently foreign to pose a slew of valuable questions: What was this album? What did its hybrid sound say about the evolution of tradition, the rigidity of identity, and the permeability of the boundaries between communities? Most important, why had no one told us about this before? If they played this at synagogue, we never would have left.

One discovery led to another. We soon found the Moog synthesizer experiments of Gershon Kingsley, the belting pyrotechnics of Shoshana Damari, and the entrepreneurial

Benny Goodman
Benny Goodman Combos
Columbia, early 1950s

The Lieber-Stoller Big Band
Yakety Yak
Atlantic, 1960s

Ruth Rubin
The Old Country
Folkways, 1958

El Avram Group
Any Time of the Year
Monitor Records, 1968

showmanship of Moishe Oysher. It turns out there were psychedelic Jewish folk gods, groovy disco cantors who wore turtleneck sweaters, Korean singers who knew every word of "Exodus," mambo wizards who held court in the Catskills, jazz legends who did *Fiddler on the Roof* medleys, Hasidic prog rockers, and Jews who made funk albums about slavery. There were albums for Jewish suburban house parties and albums for Jewish aerobics and albums for Jewish wars and albums for Jewish death. There were albums that wondered "What is a Jew?" and "Why do Jews laugh?" There were Israeli soldiers doing Broadway scissor kicks over the turrets of tanks. There were film stars singing into hand grenades. There was Charlton Heston reading the Old Testament.

Finding this music felt like discovering a forgotten kingdom of sound. Every album we rescued became part of the process of piecing together a past; every visit to a record store became an exercise in identity archaeology. The world of the Jewish LP is a lost world. The LPs that do survive are tombstones, artifacts, messages in bottles. But we also believe that they are crystal balls. For us, finding them was not simply about shedding light on an obscured Jewish past, but shedding light on our own futures, on who we would become.

And so began our personal quest to find more of these gems and build a homemade archive of Jewish-American history, one made up entirely of LP covers. We started a blog, posting about the albums we found and doing everything we could to uncover stories about the performers who had recorded them. The response was immediate and exhilarating. We received an avalanche of boxes stuffed with LPs from attics across the country, often arriving with scribbled notes thanking us for saving them from a trip to the town dump and expressing gratitude that there was someone out there who had a use for them. We reveled in their covers and devoured the liner notes as if we were piecing together the Dead Sea Scrolls.

Our garages began to fill up—all that presence, all that history. To fill the gaps in our rapidly growing collections, we began to spend nights addictively combing eBay, competing with each other to uncover ever more dramatic finds. We began to track down the performers themselves to record the stories behind their music. We phoned them up like teenagers stalking their pop heroes. Soon enough, it felt as though neither of us had a friend under the age of eighty. Along the way, we were blessed to find two remarkable and committed music experts who shared our passions, David

Katznelson and Courtney Holt. Together, we cofounded Reboot Stereophonic, a nonprofit record label determined to mend the silences of Jewish American history (our motto: "History sounds different when you know where to start listening"). Our goal was to rerelease this lost vinyl, rescuing the stories of the pioneering Jewish performers and their music from being buried alive. Reboot Stereophonic began to bring a lost world into focus, restoring to their rightful place the legacies of the artists we met.

As amazing as all the music was to us, the LP cover art held its own magic. While some take weekends to hit Vegas, play golf, or go hunting, we spent as much time as we could in Boca Raton, Florida. It became our Shangri-la —the place Jewish vinyl goes to die. We passed days in Goodwill stores, returning home weighed down with boxes of records still reeking of mothballs and air-conditioned condos. It was there that we encountered the Judaica Sound Archives of Florida Atlantic University, where Nathan Tinanoff and his devoted staff generously opened their collection to us— thousands of LPs, shelf after shelf filled with discarded cardboard and vinyl that we gushed over like scientists marveling at new specimens.

What you hold in your hands is an attempt to share what we've found so far and to unleash some of the stories that these LP covers tell. This is a sample of what we've collected, a found history of Jewish-American life. The LPs are representations, not social facts, but what they represent is massive: a history of Jewish life in America not found in newsreels, history books, or organizational archives. This is history from the bottom up, a people's history unwoven from the albums owned, cherished, and later discarded by ordinary folks who just happen to be our grandparents and parents, and others like them—a dying generation of Jewish-Americans whose stories are still waiting to be told. Yet they also speak of the opposite, of the stories that are no longer told, the subplots and narrative twists that have been edited out of history. Part of the thrill of collecting these albums has been finding the lost fragments that fit the story we have inherited and those that instead undermine it, challenge it, and ultimately transform it.

These albums belonged to people who celebrated with them, dreamed with them, and mourned with them. Some came from the same big American record labels that released Perry Como and Jimi Hendrix, some came from the dozens of small Jewish record labels that were still in operation through the 1970s. In collecting them, what we found were

STREISAND SUPERMAN

Barbra Streisand
Streisand Superman
Columbia, 1977

WHAT IT SOUNDS LIKE

Ann Powers on Barbra Streisand's "Lullaby for Myself" from *Streisand Superman*

A set-piece for the swinging, lonely seventies, "Lullaby for Myself" was written by Streisand's regular collaborator, Rupert Holmes, the man forever associated with another sonic icon of the wife-swapping era—"Escape (the Pina Colada Song)." This ballad, sung with typical attention to the dramatic build by Babs, is a more subtle, cynical version of "My Heart Belongs to Me," her biggest hit on *Superman* and another tale of how women's liberation squashed romance. While that song has the lush, enveloping quality of a disco-era ballad, "Lullaby" is frankly theatrical, hinting at the future turn Holmes would take as a Tony Award–winning playwright.

There's a setup, signaled by a tinkling Rhodes keyboard, in which Barbra announces the bland (and, we immediately suspect, false) contentment of single life. Then comes the build, cushioned by strings and energized by a rockish kick drum. The lyrics' reference to pork chops abandoned hints at the Fifth Dimension's 1970 hit "One Less Bell to Answer"—this song's obvious precursor—but while Marilyn McCoo stayed in the kitchen, Babs takes it to the bath, and a climactic image of not getting her back rubbed in the tub. Streisand's vocal, transforming from a scoff into one of her patented vibratoless long notes, hints at what she might be able to reach with that solitary hand.

The punch line comes when that intimate piano tinkle reasserts itself and she admits that she would like a man to share her unstructured day. It's a bit disappointing, but this isn't a liberatory pop song. It's theater, and it needs that little turn toward pathos to close its book. Streisand, of course, turns the lock with grace.

Jews eager to maintain tradition and preserve memory amid the unprecedented freedoms of the United States, even if it meant learning Eastern European dance steps by following a diagram tucked in an LP sleeve. We found an eagerness to detail the emergence and changing role of the idea of Israel as a national homeland, as well as a desire to document, and often celebrate, interactions with other ethnic communities in the mix of American life (particularly African Americans and Latinos). We found different approaches to Old World nostalgia and countless hints of just how heavy the influence of America has been on the religious teachings and beliefs of Judaism. The LPs also provide a window into the Jewish role in the development of American popular music —the absorption of vaudeville, burlesque, and Yiddish song traditions into jazz, swing, rock and roll, folk, mambo, and salsa. It's a tug of war as old as Ellis Island: insider ethnicity rubbing up against the tempting harmonies of assimilation in the midst of America's multicultural soup. In the end, what we found were stories about America, about immigrant assimilation, class mobility, and political liberalism, about the rise of mass culture, the invention of the suburb, the hippie boom of the sixties, and the battle for civil rights.

Little did we know that the story of the LP is itself a Jewish story. The first commercial audio-playback machine, the gramophone, was invented by a German Jew, Emile Berliner, in the late 1800s. The first long-playing 33⅓ rpm records were invented by Peter Carl Goldmark, a Hungarian Jewish immigrant who worked for the Columbia Broadcasting Systems. The Jewish head of Columbia Records, Edward Wallerstein, turned the LP into a commercial reality. The idea of adorning the LPs with cover art was the brainchild of Columbia's first art director, Alex Steinweiss, the son of Latvian and Polish Jewish immigrants who grew up on New York's Lower East Side. Soon he was designing for artists who just happened to be of various Jewish persuasions: the Russian André Kostelanetz, the Danish Victor Borge (né Børge Rosenbaum), the Tennessean-via-Russia Dinah Shore (née Frances Rose Shore), Queens-bred Richard Rodgers, and Manhattan-bred Oscar Hammerstein II.

Here's the thing: We knew who Neil Sedaka was, but we didn't have a clue about El Avram.

Look at the cover of *Neil Sedaka with the Tokens*—a perfect portrait of a Brooklyn-raised Jewish-American teenager trained in classical music who went on to become one of the archi-

Bobby Silver and Orchestra
Jewish
Cameo, 1960

Various
Jewish-American Songs for the Jet Set
Tikva, 1960s

Leo Fuld
Self-titled
Tikva, 1960s

Ruach Orchestra
The Torah Connection
National Conference of Synagogue Youth, 1982

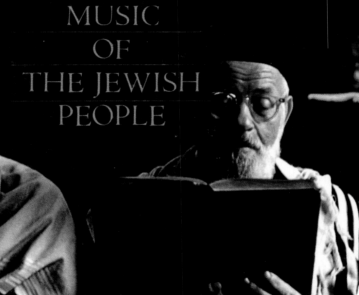

NEW IMPROVED FULL DIMENSIONAL STEREO

Leo Roth {tenor} / Leipzig Synagogue Choir / Werner Buschnakowski {organ}
Members of the Leipzig Radio Symphony Orchestra conducted by Werner Sander

Traditional Melodies of Home and Synagogue

MUSIC
OF
THE JEWISH
PEOPLE

Leo Roth and Leipzig Synagogue Choir
Music of the Jewish People
Capitol, 1957

tects of the midcentury American pop song. Sedaka is an urban sophisticate, fresh-faced in a turtleneck, his tweed blazer thrown over his shoulder. No black hats and gray beards here. At eighteen, he moved into 1650 Broadway, the legendary Brill Building and the digs of Aldon Music, Don Kirshner's publishing empire, which transformed the lessons of Tin Pan Alley into the new formulas of pop, R & B, and rock and roll. And as with Tin Pan Alley's consortium of immigrant Jews banging out songs that smelted working-class urban Jewishness into glitzy pop universalism, the Brill Building was another Jewish hit factory. In 1958, Sedaka and his writing partner, Howard Greenfield, merged twelve-bar blues and a little Hector Villa-Lobos to create "Stupid Cupid," a perky popabilly tune made famous by Connie Francis, then the most mainstream of mainstream pop stars.

Sedaka and Greenfield, of course, weren't alone at the Brill Building. They were joined by a talent-rich cadre of other young, secular Jews—Carole King, Gerry Goffin, Jeff Barry, Ellie Greenwich, Barry Mann, Doc Pomus, Cynthia Weil—who spent their days writing songs, usually for non-Jews to sing. In most cases, the songs went to African American performers: Goffin and King gave the Shirelles "Will You Love Me Tomorrow?" which made them the first girl group ever to land a number-one hit, and Greenwich and Barry put "Da Doo Ron Ron" in the mouth of the Crystals with the help of boy-genius Phil Spector (may his reputation rest in peace), who got his first guitar for his bar mitzvah. And of course, there were Jerry Lieber and Mike Stoller, those key architects of the fifties rock and R & B sound who gave the Drifters, the Coasters, and Ben E. King their biggest hits.

These stories have been told so many times that they've become commonplace in the annals of American musical history, not to mention a favorite theme of "spot the Jew" music books. Jews *are* pop music. There was Tin Pan Alley (Jewish) and vaudeville (pretty much Jewish) and rock and roll (secretly Jewish) and soon enough Paul Simon ("The 59th Street Bridge Song" was actually on our Hebrew school curriculum) and Barbra, Barry, and the other Neil (Jewish, Jewish, Jewish). And then there's Burt Bacharach and Lou Reed, the Ramones, and Kiss and Blondie (OK, just the guitarist) and David Lee Roth and yes, the Beastie Boys. Follow the thread and you end up with American pop music's greatest hits all having some connection to a string of Jewish musical chameleons who turned their immigrant pasts or Lower East Side childhoods or suburban doom into brilliant pop alchemy that became the soundtrack for the twentieth century.

It's a great story and mostly a true one, but it's not the only one. What about the Jews who didn't land on the pop charts? What *about* El Avram?

Avram Grobard was a former Israeli paratrooper living in New York City who sang in Spanish, Greek, Italian, Arabic, Japanese, English, Yiddish, and Hebrew. He opened his first Manhattan club in 1967. A chain soon followed. El Avram's clubs aimed to be a veritable underground railroad for the flood of Israeli and Middle Eastern acts attempting to make it big in America. As he put it in one of his albums' liner notes, the clubs were "a downtown bouillabaisse of Mediterranean condiments—an Israeli owner, an Armenian oud player, an Israeli Arab chef in the kitchen, and Greek, Italian, Spanish, and French music in the air." The bouillabaisse had Spanish ingredients to begin with—the club was previously El Chico, a Latin music hub with a bull's head and a sombrero hanging over the stage (Avram Grobard became "El Avram" as an homage to El Chico).

On his 1960s LP, *Any Time of the Year*, Avram did songs like the Israeli "Bashana Haba'ah" (the title track), the Armenian "Kale, Kale," and the Russian "Kazachok." On the cover of the LP—with his chest hair proudly sprouting beneath his denim jumpsuit—he looks ready to merge tambourine-slapped and dumbek-drummed Israeli folk traditions with American love-ins and flower power.

We were ready for Neil Sedaka. But having grown up with the invasion of Lebanon and the Intifada, we were shocked that there was once a market for a joyous Israeli paratrooper who sang in Japanese, adopted a Spanish nickname, opened a Manhattan nightclub for fans of Mediterranean music, recorded a Passover commercial with a Texas cowboy (it's true, we have the seven-inch single), and then released a series of LPs of Israeli hits while dressed for a long night at a seventies disco. Where had El Avram—this groovy, optimistic, and surprising face of Israel—been all our lives?

By the end of the 1960s, you didn't have to be Jewish to know about "Tradition!" The astronomical popularity of *Fiddler on the Roof*— first the Broadway show, then the Hollywood blockbuster—cemented a pretty clear picture of what the Jewish past looked like: Old World Poverty, the Musical! "Tradition!" became a Jewish punch line, an idea that immediately conjured up dancing milkmen and Marc Chagall paintings. It was as if the Jewish past had been constructed, staged, and shot for the masses, a gold standard frozen in time.

We prefer another approach to tradition, one on loan from philosopher Gershom Sholem. "There is a life of tradition that does not merely consist of conservative preservation," he wrote, "the constant continuation of the spiritual and cultural possessions of a community. There is such a thing as a treasure hunt within tradition, which creates a living relationship to tradition and to which much of what is best in current Jewish consciousness is indebted, even where it was—and is—expressed outside the framework of orthodoxy."

Welcome to our own treasure hunt within tradition, our own living relationship to what's come before us and what lies ahead, to what we know and what we are still seeking to find.

Roger Bennett
Josh Kun
May, 2008
www.trailofourvinyl.com

CHAPTER ONE

MEN'S WEARHOUSE: THE CHANGING SARTORIAL STYLES OF THE GREAT CANTORS

Bing Crosby. Michael Jackson. Elvis Presley. Frank Sinatra. Four of the best-selling artists of all time have been male solo acts. It should not be surprising, then, that the Mosaic equivalent, the cantor, dominated the early Jewish record market too. The sheer number of these studio liturgical recordings is a reflection of the massive fan base who once hungered for these gems. They were consumed by both the observant—those who adored synagogue so much that the only way they could survive between the evening and morning services was to spin some cantorial vinyl in their own homes—and those who no longer attended synagogue at all but missed the holy harmonies enough to covet them in private.

The American version of the cantorial tradition began amid the new prosperity of the late nineteenth century. American Jews then decided that nothing would add an extra layer of polish to the synagogues they were building more than importing a legendary Eastern European–trained cantor on a huge contract. The mountain of cash typically expended was worth every penny, for crowds would throng the building to hear these living symbols of the religious tradition air their pipes in their new settings of American affluence. The cantors were elevated to rock-star status and left to navigate the uncharted and treacherous waters of being both holy men and showmen.

The 1920s and '30s were the golden age of cantorial music, and the album covers capture the pomp and grandeur of the time. At first

Jan Peerce
Cantoral Masterpieces
Vanguard, 1962

Yossele Rosenblatt
A Concert with Yossele Rosenblatt, Volume II
Greater Recording Co., 1973

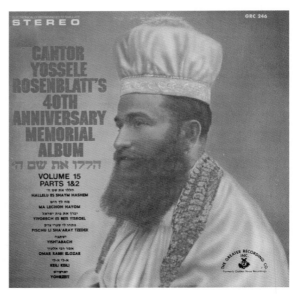

Yossele Rosenblatt
Cantor Yossele Rosenblatt's 40th
Anniversary Memorial Album
Greater Recording Co., 1973

David Roitman
The Best Cantoral Works of Cantor David Roitman
Greater Recording Co., 1966

Various
The Great "Zoger" Chazonim, Volume I
Greater Recording Co., 1970

blush, the performers, a hirsute bunch in their flowing robes and distinctive headwear, resemble the living emblems of piety and tradition that one would expect. But a closer look reveals the signs of the creeping commerciality of the period. The cantors are almost too meticulously groomed and well fed; their tailored suits and general finery hint of the ballooning salaries they were raking in. The career of Yossele Rosenblatt stands as a fine example. Rosenblatt was a sensation from the age of twelve in his Ukrainian hometown of Biela Tserkov, where he developed a signature sobbing sound. He was eventually lured to New York, when a synagogue in Harlem made him the world's highest-paid cantor, with an annual income of over $5,000 a year. On the cover of *A Concert with Yossele Rosenblatt, Volume II,* Rosenblatt stands proudly upright in a three-piece suit, clutching an umbrella. The jewelry draped across his belly is a handy symbol of the conflict between the sacred and the commercial.

These superstar cantors were caught in a bind. The more popular they became as showmen, the more they eroded the traditions around them. The first step to becoming a recording artist was becoming a performing artist. There was a resulting shift from the participatory culture of the synagogue where everyone knew all the words and melodies to a realm in which congregants came to marvel at what they heard and chime in with the odd Amen. The service became less about sanctity and more about spectacle. A legendary Rosenblatt tale recalls one performance when he coaxed a round of applause, midprayer, from his congregants, behavior previously unheard of in an Orthodox synagogue. That was more suitable for Carnegie Hall, where he had also begun to appear, singing not "Hine Ma Tov" but Verdi's "Questa o quella." Ultimately, the allure of the vaudeville circuit pulled him away from the synagogue completely. The financial reward for performing between silent movies and circus freaks was too great to ignore, but once talkies began to proliferate, his career died almost overnight (save for a small cameo role alongside Al Jolson in *The Jazz Singer,* a film that made the secular-spiritual battle of the American cantor into its Hollywood plotline), and he passed away in poverty in 1933, his life a symbol of the conflict between the sacred and the profane, the synagogue and the cinema, the Jewish and the universal.

Cantor Pierre Pinchik symbolizes these tensions on the cover of his *Two Sides of Pinchik,* where he is a cantor divided: Pinchik the pious in cantorial garb and Pinchik the civilian in his

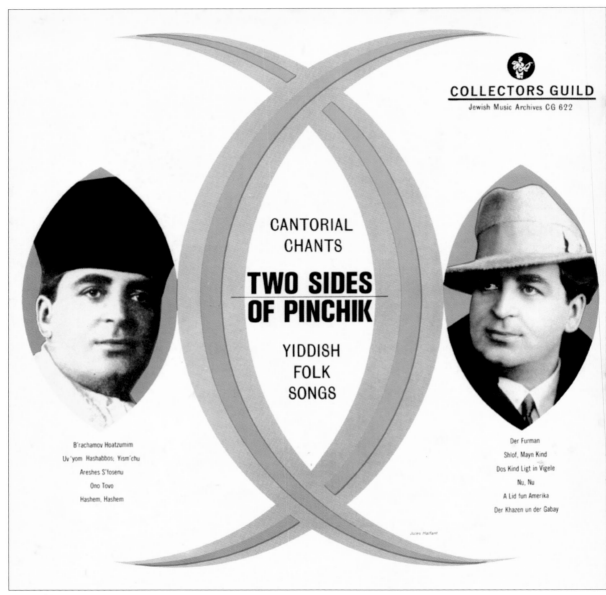

Pierre Pinchik
Two Sides of Pinchik
Collectors Guild, 1962

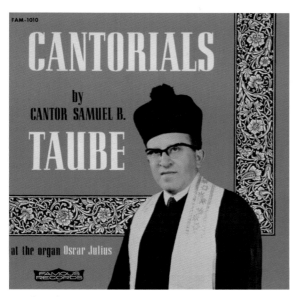

Samuel B. Taube
Cantorials by Cantor Samuel B. Taube
Famous Records, c. 1960

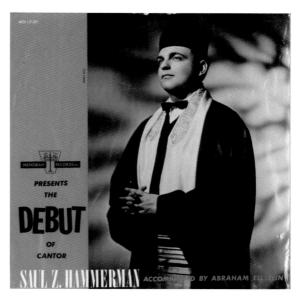

Saul Z. Hammerman
The Debut of Cantor Saul Z. Hammerman
Menorah, c. 1960

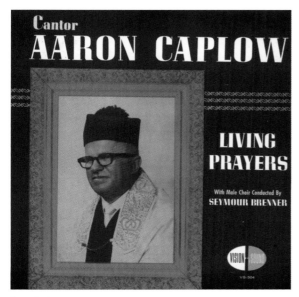

Aaron Caplow
Living Prayers
Vision and Sound, c. 1960

Jo Amar
Oriental Songs
Hed-Arzi, c. 1960

rakishly tilted hat. The cantorial Jekyll and Hyde images are separated by two giant blue parentheses, the cantor and the showman left to exist in connected but separate worlds. This tension was accelerated by the postwar building boom, in which a third of America's Jews moved out to the suburbs in the 1950s. Judaism, which had been a quintessentially urban culture in America, underwent the equivalent of an extreme makeover to incorporate the suburban values of consumption, mobility, and leisure. Ground was broken on hundreds of synagogues across the country, reinventing the cantor's place of work as a temple—grand palaces of Judaism desperate to compete with everything else the suburbs offered within driving distance. The bimah was raised like a stage, the seating was set out theater-style, and the synagogue gift stores were stocked with cantorial records in the hope that, just as on Broadway, the audience would want to take home a memento of the performance. But the covers of the records suggest that the sales were slender. The clean-shaven look has replaced the traditional beard, the ritual shawls, tallithim, are more discreet, and most significantly, all of the cantors look as though they buy their suits off the rack, a telltale sign that there is not enough money left in the cantorial game for the bespoke tailoring of yore.

Some artists, like Jan Peerce, go so far as to pose by the scrolls of a Torah as if they need to give the Jewish consumer a none-too-subtle memory jog as to the album's content.

The iconic cantor of this generation was Richard Tucker, born Ruvn Ticker, an esteemed opera singer who maintained his cantorial career as a side project even while starring in *Aïda* at the Met. Tucker had a prestigious cantorial output but also cropped up alongside Danny Kaye and Sammy Davis Jr. on the Goodyear Tire and Rubber Company's *Great Songs of Christmas by Great Artists of Our Time*. His contribution was "O Little Town of Bethlehem," a solid sign that the real cantor cash was to be made within the universal.

As the cantorial market struggled, it began to diversify. Records of note included a handful by women, including the great Shaindele Di Chazante (literally, Shaindele the Cantoress), who found fame, if not fortune, in the postwar years as a touring star despite the fact that her gender kept her from finding an actual synagogue pulpit. She couldn't sing to a congregation in a synagogue, but the LP opened up other possible audiences. Her regal cover highlights the shifting gender politics of Judaism at midcentury, when women were increasingly becoming the key caretakers of religous customs within the family.

Yeshiva Student Chorus
New Yeshiva Songs
Tikva, c. 1960

The Singers of Israel
A Cantoral Concert
Tikva, c. 1960

Fraydele Oysher and Her Daughter Marilyn
Songs My Brother Moishe Sang
Tikva, c. 1960

Hershele Leibovitz
Hershele Sings
Greater Recording Co., 1966

Shaindele
Shaindele Sings the Songs of Her People
Margot Records, c. 1950

Within the synagogue, however, women were not the only minority act. A market also emerged for Sephardic cantorial pyrotechnics. Few were more popular or more dashing than the ever cool Jo Amar, the Moroccan Prince, whose mastery of mizrahi intonation dazzled American audiences.

As synagogue audiences started to evaporate, opportunity remained for those entrepreneurial enough to perform in places Jews continued to attend. A handsomely cloaked cantor gazes lovingly at the new promised land of a Catskills resort on the cover of *Herman Malamood at the Concord with the Concord Symphony Orchestra*. Another singer, Bela Herskovits, leveraged an appearance on the holy of holies, network television, to make his album *The "This Is Your Life" Cantor*. The liner notes show that the solitary television appearance did wonders for his confidence. "Bela Herskovits has made a name for himself, a career more brilliant than that attained by any other cantor in history. He is facile in seventeen languages." Herskovitz, ever the pop cantor, even had film and comedy star Eddie Cantor share the stage with him when he played Carnegie Hall. The act was billed as Two Cantors.

By the 1970s the cantorial market was left to those like the old craftsman Jan Peerce and LPs like *Jan Peerce Today!* (the exclamation point inadvertently suggesting surprise that he was still alive). By donning a velvet tux and ruffled dress shirt, the Eastern European–born Herschel Fox resembles a nightclub entertainer more than a cantor. Those who believe that children are our future will be happy to know that by the 1980s, yeshiva boy bands dominated what was left of the market with their high-pitched renditions of songs popularized by the great cantors nearly a century before them. These male groups all have their different look replete with color-coordinated shirts and beanies. But it is the special flourishes that set them apart—such as the conductor inexplicably donning a gorilla outfit on *Shmuel Borger Presents Amudai Shaish Boys Choir*. Then there's *The London School of Jewish Song*, an album cover so desperate to save the faith that it tries to stand in for an actual worshipper. It comes complete with its own dangling ritual fringes.

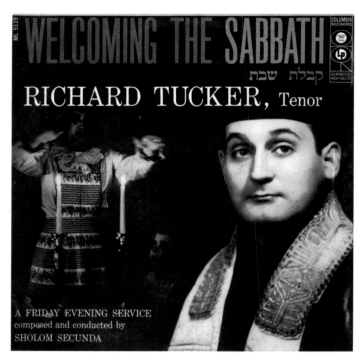

Richard Tucker
Welcoming the Sabbath
Columbia, 1956

Various
*Great Songs of Christmas by Great
Artists of Our Time, Volume 5*
Columbia, 1965

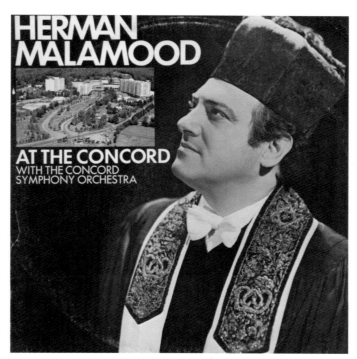

Herman Malamood
*Herman Malamood at the Concord
with the Concord Symphony
Orchestra*
Released by the Concord Hotel, 1977

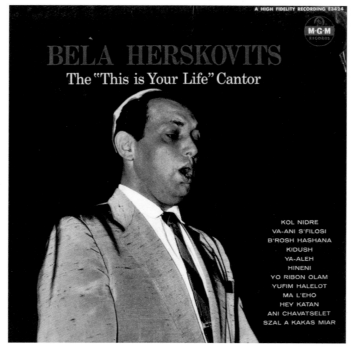

Bela Herskovits
The "This Is Your Life" Cantor
MGM, 1957

YERACHMIEL
BEGUN'S

Miami

CHOIR BOYS

VICTORY ENTEBBE · NEGINAH SYMPHONY ORCHESTRA

KT 1800

Miami Choir Boys
Victory Entebbe
Kee-Tov, 1977

Josh Rosenfeld on "Entebbe" by the Miami Boys Choir from *Miami Choir Boys*

This is pretty great. It exemplifies that charming unswinging version of orchestrated funk that got pretty popular there in the late seventies for a while, with instrumentation that conjures up a strange mixture of styles—*Hawaii Five-O* meets *Spartacus*, played by the Springfield Symphony Orchestra with guest appearances by the dudes who recorded the Ennio Morricone film scores, and pushed over the top by a bunch of prepubescent kids wearing white lace-front shirts and matching embroidered vests. You know—ethnic. I can't stop listening to it.

Jan Peerce
Jan Peerce Today!
Vanguard Recording Society, 1982

Moshe Taube
Cantor Moshe Taube Sings Hallal
Segué, c. 1960s

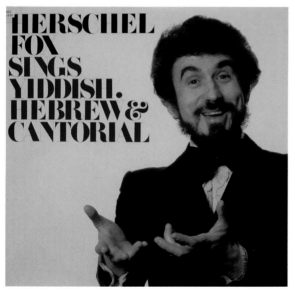

Herschel Fox
*Herschel Fox Sings Yiddish, Hebrew
& Cantorial*
Mazel, 1980

Cantor Deitell
Cantor Deitell's Best
Self-published, 1975

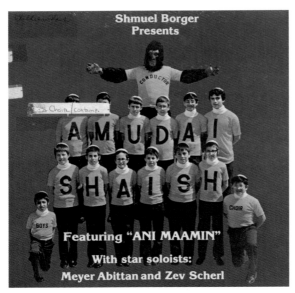

Shmuel Borger
Shmuel Borger Presents Amudai Shaish Boys Choir
Ziontalis Record Division, 1983

Moti Zingboim
Chassidic Songs
Dalton, c. 1970

Pirchei Zmirei Zion
Junior Chassidic Song Contest Nr. 2
Dalton, c. 1970

B.J.E. Children's Choir
Chicago Pirchim Sing
Musique Internationale, 1974

Yigal Y. Calek
The London School of Jewish Song
Moshe Kahan Productions, c. 1970

Sol Zim—The Original Star of David

Every musical genre can boast of its most prolific recording artist. Willie Nelson has recorded over 120 albums. Johnny Mathis has released nearly 100. In the Jewish musical world, few can touch the output of Sol Zim. Born Solomon Zimelman in Portland, Maine, a descendant of five generations of cantors, his artistry, interpretative skills, creativity, and awe-inspiring productivity have left an indelible mark on the Jewish musical landscape, supplying it with an evolving musical sound and some of its most spectacular album covers.

Zim has had a chameleonic career, recording in a number of guises on the Tikvah, Menorah, and his own Zimray record labels. He has had an on-again, off-again partnership, the Brothers Zim with his younger brother, Paul. He's been a solo artist, recording under the name Sebastian Zim during a brief dalliance with United Artists, and he made a spectacular series of holiday recordings with his own family. Cantorship was Zim's first and true love, however. He revolutionized the form with his great inventiveness and antiphonal singing—

the cantor as song leader, chanting melodies back and forth with an audience who were increasingly unable to read Hebrew. "God gave me the gift of melody," he explained proudly. "I wrote arrangements that you have heard so often in synagogue that you think they come from Sinai. They didn't. I wrote them."

For Zim, performing was the ultimate high. "I am a gladiator on stage. I am a wild man. I look and act just like Tom Jones." When his sons took him to see Kiss at Madison Square Garden, the experience changed his life.

Sol Zim

Sol Zim

Sol Zim

I was spellbound. This was wonderful musicality with a popular feel, yet there was something classical to it all. And so I began to write for the pop field, to mix the old and the new and engage the young people."

His album *David Superstar*, recorded live at the Hollis Hills Jewish Center, was the result. A scintillating package with its rock-and-roll reinvention, Zim in a trippy sweater vest, and liner notes that claim proudly that through "the ROCK MEDIA our younger generation can be reached en masse." His fans were not surprised by this new pop direction. I have always been very avant-garde, and Jews have traditionally been influenced by the music around them, so this was the perfect mix of the nostalgia of yester-year coupled with the new age of tomorrow." But Zim paid a price for his daring. "I was toma-toed off stage during a perform-ance at the Cantors Association. I did not care though. I drew sol-ace in the fact that I was twenty years ahead of them all."

The portfolio of albums here is a testament to this fact. One constant is Zim's striking style and persona, which is always to the fore. I am a clothes bug. I love to dress secular—especial-ly in paisley—which reflects that my arrangements are secular but the music is Jewish." Jewelry was a critical detail too. His signature gold chai necklace was handmade. "My fans always wanted to kiss my Star of David. The high priest— the *cohen gadol*—was always my look." His personal favorite covers are the ones with his family. "For all my success, they are my greatest thrill. My wife is a gorgeous woman. She looks like Zsa Zsa Gabor."

The Zimel Brothers
Sing Chassidic Melodies
Tikva, c. 1960

The Brothers Zim
The Joy of Shabbos
Zimray, 1977

The Brothers Zim
The Brothers Zim in Concert Singing Jewish Nostalgia
Zimray, 1978

CHAPTER TWO

THE YIDDISH ARE COMING: HOW VINYL KEPT A DYING LANGUAGE ALIVE

We both grew up in households that used Yiddish words as punch lines, punctuation, and insult. We knew who was a schmuck, what it felt like to *shvitz* when the A/C wasn't on full blast, and knew things weren't so good when an *oy* was exhaled with a shake of the head. As it is for just about anyone weaned on network television and Hollywood films, we knew the meaning of Yiddish words mostly because of context, because they were surrounded by English. As languages go, Yiddish is surely an odd case—a language that is constantly used and referenced and yet truly known by so few.

The reason, we were always told, was that Yiddish was a dying, or perhaps already dead, language. No matter where we looked, the story of Yiddish never seemed to have a happy ending. It was a "back in the days" language, a "once upon a time" language, what they spoke back in the Old Country. It was a language that belonged to Eastern European village life, to hunched old men in tattered black coats and pudgy old ladies boiling borscht. There was once a flourishing Yiddish literary world with rich traditions of theater and music, and when Jews made their way to America at the turn of the twentieth century, all of those arts were reborn in the urban mix of places like the Lower East Side. In the 1920s, there were so many Yiddish speakers in New York City that the Yiddish daily newspaper the *Forward* outsold the *New York Times*. Then the Holocaust cut the number of the world's Yiddish speakers in half. Then Stalin purged Yiddish from the Soviet Union. Then Israel chose Hebrew as the new Jewish state's official language. In America, after the glory days of vaude-

Selma Rich Brody
Children, Let Us Speak Yiddish
Strand, 1962

Commission on Jewish Affairs
Invitation to Yiddish
Released by the Commission on
Jewish Affairs, 1962

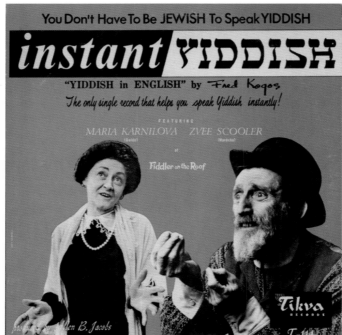

Fred Kogos
Instant Yiddish
Tikva, 1966

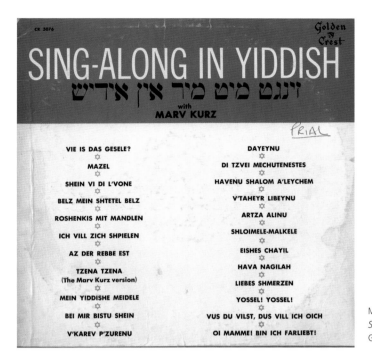

Marv Kurz
Sing-along in Yiddish
Golden Crest, 1962

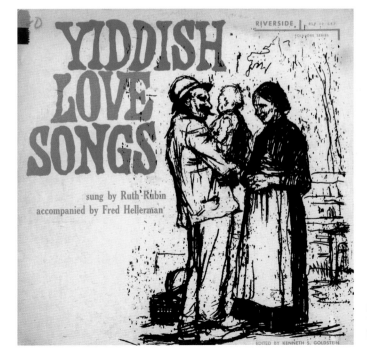

Ruth Rubin
Yiddish Love Songs
Riverside Records, 1957

ville and the Yiddish theater, hundreds of thousands of upwardly mobile American Jews gradually chose mastering English over keeping their *mamaloshen* alive.

This was not the gradual dwindling of a language over time, but a quick-fire decimation of a language in a matter of a decade. As scholar Jeffrey Shandler has written, where once Yiddish was the default language of the world's Jews—to be Jewish meant to speak Yiddish—after World War II it had become optional, one of many tools available to build, and rebuild, Jewish identity amid the uncertainties of the Diaspora.

This seems true, but as we started collecting LPs that featured Yiddish, it became clear that for a dying language, there sure were a lot of albums being bought by living people. The market for Yiddish recordings was undoubtedly smaller than before World War II, but it hadn't vanished altogether: No record company puts out an album if they don't think money can be made. Granted, many Yiddish LPs in the postwar years were as much albums begging people to keep speaking Yiddish as they were albums actually featuring Yiddish music.

Take *Invitation to Yiddish*, the double LP that the American Jewish Congress released in 1964 complete with a 108-page manual. There is little that is actually inviting about it; it's nothing but text, all of it rendered in bar mitzvah blue and white. There are no shots of Yiddish street signs or Yiddish storefronts or Yiddish movie marquees to be found. This is an invitation to a language, not a culture or a life. The back cover reels off proclamations: "Yiddish is needed to understand your cultural background." "Yiddish is easy to learn." The LP should have been called "Speak my language—please." Its language lessons are guilt trips. One of them is even titled, "You should know something about your people."

Slightly more seductive might be *Sing-Along in Yiddish*, which features the "uniquely delightful" Marv Kurz belting some of Yiddish music's more memorable gems. Forget all that mess about learning the language, all that business about cultural heritage and maintaining ties to Jews all over the world and being able to speak to your grandparents. Here you just put the needle on the record and sing along as best you can. No guilt, no historical pressure, no cultural down payment.

The *Instant Yiddish* LP goes a step further by giving up on the Jews altogether. "You don't have to be Jewish to speak Yiddish," it beams, targeting a universal audience by including Zvee Scooler and Maria Karnilova, who, the cover reminds us, are from the cast of *Fiddler on the Roof*, the musical that turned the Jewish past into an American pasttime. If you sang along with Tevye, if you emotionally identified with all those matchmakers and poor Eastern

The Feder Sisters
Some Like It Yiddish
1959, United Artists

Jan Bart
Jan Bart Sings Yinglish
Janson Records, 1960s

Original New York Cast
Hello Solly!
Capitol, 1967

Jennie Goldstein
Mink . . . Shmink, as Long as You're Healthy
King Records, 1957

Emil Cohen
Jewish Stories & Songs
Emco, 1954

European village milkmen who dream about being rich while they dance around in rags, then why not give Yiddish a try? With Yiddish in crisis (Israeli TV even refused to translate the Eichmann trial into the language), they give the hard sell. We'll take anyone, even the Gentiles.

Yet the bulk of Yiddish LPs tends to keep the Gentiles out of the picture, being targeted at a particular niche—midcentury Jews who don't share a language as much as they share a language problem: whether to speak Yiddish or English. Speak through the past or speak for the future? Of course, for people like our grandparents, the choice was not a crisis at all, but a chance for new identities.

The Feder Sisters, a Yiddish swing duo who never made it out of the shadow of the Barry Sisters, were used to navigating both worlds. Daughters of Yiddish theater actors and hosts of their own Yiddish music radio show, Sylvia and Miriam Feder worked in vaudeville and the Catskills. The sisters admit that only *some* like it Yiddish and look happy enough about it on the cover—smiling and perfectly made-up, looking ready for a suburban Tupperware party or a weekday luncheon as much as a jazzy take on "Mazel" or "Oy Mama."

These cultural back-and-forths also show up on the cover of star tenor Jan Bart's *Jan Bart Sings Yinglish* album, where flickering Sabbath candles look out onto a view of the Manhattan skyline, the private world of Jewishness dwarfed by the cosmopolitan world that waits beyond the window. The Yinglish of the title promises a batch of bilingual tunes, but the whole album is in English. Apparently the skyline won.

Actual Yinglish albums did flourish somewhat, especially in the comedy world. Cheeky raconteur Marty Gale promises *Sexy Stories with a Yiddisha Flavor*, with titles that straddle worlds ("He Kisses a Nasty Tzizta," "I Bit Her on the Pipik"), while Emil Cohen, who immodestly bills himself as "America's foremost American-Jewish humorist," unravels his own tales about cantors, telegrams, and the Gettysburg Address that might start in English but end with Yiddish punch lines. To get the jokes you don't just have to be Jewish, you have to be "American-Jewish"—you have to belong to a community where the dualities of language and culture have become the everyday norm.

Instead of issuing Yiddish a death certificate, LPs tried to envision a new Yiddish life full of new Americanized speakers whom Leo Fuchs calls "Yiddish-Americans" on his *Shalom Pardner*. Fuchs might have once been known as the Yiddish Fred Astaire, but here he's hamming it up as a Jewish cowboy on the range, riding his horse backward with a Star of David on his cowboy hat. On the record itself, he does Yiddish classics like "Roumania, Roumania" and "Oy Volt Ich Gevolt" but leads them off with his "Yiddish-Twist." The

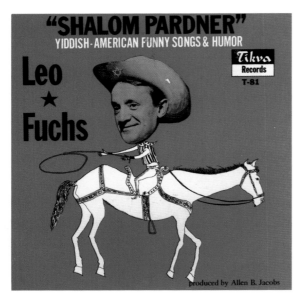

Leo Fuchs
Shalom Pardner
Tikva, 1960s

Benny Bell
Kosher Comedy
Bell Enterprises, 1958

Eli Basse
The Garden of Yeden
Rivoli Records, 1950s

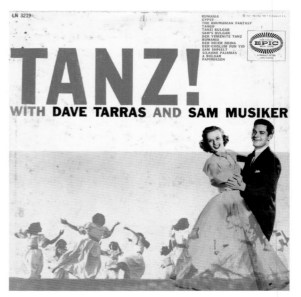

Dave Tarras and Sam Musiker
Tanz!
Epic, 1956

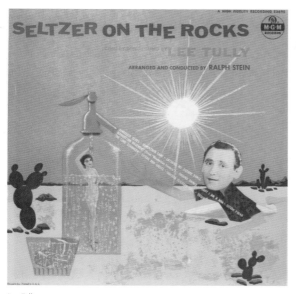

Lee Tully
Seltzer on the Rocks
MGM, 1958

Solomon Schwartz
Yiddish American Sing-a-long
London, 1967

Molly Picon
Molly Picon Sings Jewish Melodies
RCA Victor, late 1940s

Molly Picon
The Kosher Widow
Golden Crest, 1969

CARI-GALE LP #1

SEXY STORIES
WITH A
YIDDISHA FLAVOR
TOLD BY THE HAYMISHA COMEDIAN
MARTY GALE

GIVE ME A FUCHA!
THAT'S A HARD ONE
HAVE YOU GOT MATZA BALLS?
CUT OFF HIS EXHAUST PIPE
HE KISSES A NASTY TZITZA
LET HIM IN HALFWAY
TAKE IT OUT-PUT IT BACK
MISTER YENSIN
MEET MISS NAFKAWITZ
THE FLAT CHESTED GIRL
TOOCHUS ARIFF
I BIT HER ON THE PIPPIK
LAYING ON MY BACK WITH ARTHA RITIS

AND MANY OTHERS

MADE IN U.S.A

Marty Gale
Sexy Stories with a Yiddisha Flavor
Cari- Gale Records, early 1960s

Michael Wex on Marty Gale's *Sexy Stories with a Yiddisha Flavor*

It's my early-sixties wet dream of Yiddish-speaking maturity in precleanup Las Vegas. I'm an Italian-suited sophisticate who has remained true to his roots. I've got a highball in one hand, a bottle blonde on the other, and I'm explaining Yiddish obscenities to a roomful of eager listeners whose addiction to delicatessen is killing them slowly—but they don't care.

It could only happen in America: I'm married to a brunette and have never been to Vegas, but all the rest is as described above. And my wife's on her way to the drugstore to buy some Lady Clairol.

song starts in a mild klezmer mode and then suddenly Fuchs leaps off the horse and into rock and roll as he "twists, twists, twists" the night away.

Many of Fuchs's colleagues from the old days of Yiddish theater also received plenty of attention on LPs, though on many soundtrack recordings (*The Kosher Widow*, *Bei Mir Bist Du Schoen*) they worked hard to adapt to the changing cultural and linguistic alliances of their audiences by keeping most of the title in English. *Yiddish American Sing-A-Long* is full of Yiddish theater tunes but replaces the stage with a fiery gold menorah. Once the product of a specific dramatic tradition, here the music is more valuable as the score to a generalized, one-size-fits-all Jewishness.

Yiddish theater star Molly Picon makes a similar move when she pops up as a guest on *Jewish Folk Songs*, which features a pairing emblematic of Jewish music's midcentury double life—Sholom Secunda and Catskills comic turned *New York Post* columnist Joey Adams (who, the liner notes tell us, has been a hit "from the   jungles of Laos to the bar mitzvahs of Brooklyn"). In his tux with a silver bow tie, Secunda is ready for a night at the theater. In his gold-buttoned blazer, Adams—who goofs around more on the cover than he does on any of the tunes inside, which he delivers with an earnest and oozing nostalgia—looks ready for a night at Grossinger's.

One of our favorite finds has been a whole subgenre of Yiddish LPs that speak directly to the language's struggle for survival: the "Songs My Mother Taught Me" collections. Here Yiddish is not a public language but a private ritual carried out between accent-laden fathers and mothers and their restless accent-free American kids. Comedian Patsy Abbot puts her own spin on it on *Yiddish Songs My Mother Never Taught Me*. With her Old World *yiddishe momme* in an apron and young blond Patsy with her hair and eyelashes done (she used to be Goldie Schwartz), the two may sit at the same kitchen table surrounded by all the accoutrements of midcentury secular Jewishness (rye bread, Dr. Brown's Cel-Ray soda, kosher salami), but on the Yiddish continuum they're at opposite ends.

Whether it's the child singing about the Jewish mother (cue one of the countless versions of the legendary "My Yiddishe Momma") or the Jewish mother teaching the child Yiddish songs, the questions are always the same: Are the songs remembered by the kids? Can American entertainment withstand blasts of Mama's immigrant past?

In our own ways, we inherited this legacy. We were taught some songs and some words, but Yiddish never became our language. Instead, it became the sound of a history that we belonged to, the sound of cultural memory itself. All of these Yiddish LPs put faces to the *oy veys* and *meshuganahs* of our youth and make connecting to the past as easy as pulling a record off the shelf.

Leo Fuld
Mazzel
CBS Records, 1966

David Eshet
The Latest Yiddish Songs
DRG Recordings, 1960s

Jeannette La Bianca
La Bianca
Tikva, 1960s

Joey Adams and Sholom Secunda
Jewish Folk Songs
Roulette, 1964

Leo Fuchs
Bei Mir Bistu Schoen
Decca, 1963

Various
Let's Sing Yiddish
Roulette, 1966

Joel Gray
Songs My Father Taught Me
Capitol, 1967

Rose Padden
A Mama Sings a Liedele
Apollo, 1960

Patsy Abbott; Ben Jaffe
Yiddish Songs Mama Never Taught Me
Roulette, 1964

The 4 Bursteins
With a Jewish Flavor
Famous Records, c. 1960

Zero Mostel
Songs My Mother Never Sang
Vanguard, 1966

t ranks as one of the greatest name changes in the history of Jewish music. In 1937, the Bronx's own Clara and Minnie Bagelman, already doing their thing as a Yiddish singing duo aptly named the Bagelman Sisters, heard the uber-vanilla Andrews Sisters' English-language hit with the Yiddish theater staple "Bei Mir Bist Du Schoen." So they decided to get a little more vanilla themselves. Overnight, they went from Clara and Minnie to Claire and Merna, from Bagelman to Barry.

The name job did the trick, and by 1938 the Barry Sisters were the vocal stars of the *Yiddish Melodies in Swing* radio show, broadcast weekly on WHN in New York. During this Manischewitz-sponsored program, part of the *American Jewish Hour* series, Sam Medoff led the Swingtet band that featured klezmer giant Dave Tarras on clarinet and together with the Barry Sisters on the microphones, they gave Yiddish folk songs a face-lift with what the show dubbed "merry modern rhythms." Songs like "Reb Duvidel" and "Eli Melech" were "rocked solid" and "made gold" by infusions of downbeats and Harlem swing as Claire and Merna crooned, belted, and harmonized atop it all like hip supper-club stars. The show ran until 1955, and the Barry Sisters became synonymous with the jazz-meets-klezmer mash-ups of the Yiddish swing craze.

Singing in both Yiddish and English, covering both classic Yiddish tunes and contemporary jazz and pop hits (even "I'm an Old Cowhand [from the Rio Grande]" and "Mame"), the Barry Sisters became the Yiddish pop world's biggest crossover success story. On *The Barry Sisters Sing*, they

The Barry Sisters
Our Way
Mainstream, 1973

The Barry Sisters
Something Spanish
ABC, 1966

The Barry Sisters
Side by Side
Roulette, 1960

The Barry Sisters
A Time to Remember
ABC, 1967

played up their roots in the Yiddish music world by posing behind a table set for a Friday night Shabbat dinner, and on another, *A Time to Remember*, they play urban sophisticates, out for a Manhattan spree that would go way past sundown.

Their LPs were full of the ethnic identity swaps and secular/spiritual tugs of war that American Jews had become accustomed to by midcentury. On *At Home with the Barry Sisters*, they could be smiling Gentiles, ready for a visit from June Cleaver or Harriet Nelson. Yet they go more wittingly exotic in the Arabian Nights gowns of *We Belong Together*, the Andalusian lace of *Something Spanish*, and the red lace dresses of *Side by Side*—part Indochina, part Old West bordello. When they head out to see *Fiddler on the Roof*, Claire and Merna are in matching white mink coats and red gloves. When they get off their plane on the cover of *Shalom*—either back from their peace trip to Russia or from their stint singing for Israeli troops during the Six-Day War—they are in full-tilt pageant-queen mode, politely waving while balancing their overstuffed bouquets.

The Barry Sisters' last album together, the seventies gem *Our Way*, is admittedly our favorite. On the back cover the dynamic duo are draped in matching mink stoles and hats, but on the front they're dressed down in smart pantsuits in what looks to be a tony Florida condo primed for two vacationing New York snowbirds. No Shabbat candles here, but there is enough raised velvet wallpaper to turn even "Raindrops Keep Falling on My Head" into the Yiddish pop jam it was perhaps always meant to be.

The Barry Sisters
The World of the Barry Sisters
Roulette, 1956

The Barry Sisters
At Home with the Barry Sisters
Roulette, 1958

The Barry Sisters
We Belong Together
Roulette, 1961

The Barry Sisters
The Barry Sisters in Israel
Recorded Live

CHAPTER THREE

GO DOWN MOSES:
THE MUSIC OF BLACK-JEWISH
RELATIONS

As soon as we started telling people that this book would have a chapter devoted to the musical relationship between blacks and Jews, the usual response went something like, "How many Sammy Davis Jr. albums *are* there?" There are, as a matter of fact, plenty, but only one makes it onto these pages (the rapturous cover of *I Gotta Be Me* was just too hard to pass up). We wanted to include our favorite recording by the world's most famous African-American Jewish celebrity but it's not an LP, it's a super-rare 45-rpm single of Sammy singing "songs for Americans to live by" produced by the Anti-Defamation League of B'Nai B'rith.

Sammy is just the tip of the iceberg. As long as there has been American popular music,

blacks and Jews have been somewhere in the middle of it all. From the synergies of Tin Pan Alley that gave us George and Ira Gershwin's *Porgy and Bess* and an LP like *Billy Eckstine and Sarah Vaughan Sing the Best of Irving Berlin* to Benny Goodman and Artie Shaw insisting on integrated swing bands, from Barry Goldberg's earnest blues foray *Two Jews Blues* to George Jessel still managing to be proud of calling himself *The Last of the Minstrel Men*. These LPs bear witness to some of the key currents of black-Jewish relations: the cross-cultural collaboration, the bonding over common histories of oppression and suffering, and the accusations of theft and exploitation.

Did Irving Berlin steal from black ragtime

LN 1128 ® "Epic" Marca Reg. "CBS" T M. Printed in U S A

LONG PLAYING
EPIC
A PRODUCT OF CBS

THE IMMORTALS — JOLSON AND CANTOR

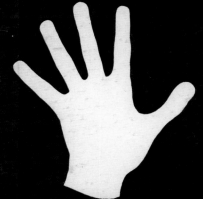

Al Jolson and Eddie Cantor
The Immortals
Epic, 1955

Sammy Davis Jr.
I've Gotta Be Me
Reprise, 1967

Howard Thomashefsky
It's Tough to Be Gifted, Jewish & Black
Laff, 1972

great Lukie Johnson to come up with "Alexander's Ragtime Band"? Did Sophie Tucker try to steal "A Good Man Is Hard to Find" from black blues queen Alberta Hunter (the same Alberta Hunter who went to Israel and came back singing "Ich Hob Dich Tzufil Lieb" on *The Dick Cavett Show*)? Cab Calloway sang in Yiddish, while Louis Armstrong started scatting—on the aptly titled tune "Heebie Jeebies"—after hearing the rhythmic mumble of synagogue prayers.

The musical history of blacks and Jews is full of these forking paths. Perhaps most famous of all is the evolution of Sholom Secunda's Yiddish musical number, "Bei Mir Bist Du Schoen" ("To Me, You Are Beautiful"). After fading from its popularity on the Yiddish stage, the song was picked up by the African-American vaudeville duo Johnny and George during a Catskills gig translated into English by songwriters Sammy Cahn and Lou Levy, and handed to a trio of Lutheran blondes, the Andrews Sisters, who turned the tune into a national pop hit.

Or there's Billie Holiday's terrifying lynching lament, "Strange Fruit," which was penned by a Jew, Abel Meeropol, aka Lewis Allan, or Harold Arlen's "Stormy Weather," a Cotton Club classic that would never leave the African-American pop repertoire. The song even ended up in the able hands of the half-Jewish Willie "the Lion" Smith, who did an instrumental take on "Stormy Weather" years after tackling "Eli, Eli," a Yiddish theater tune that dates back to 1896.

"Eli, Eli" has plenty of its own lore. After being a hit for Al Jolson and cantorial star Yossele Rosenblatt, the tune became a must-cover with black artists like Duke Ellington, Ethel Waters, and Paul Robeson. So many black singers covered the song during the early part of the century that it was part of a lampoon of Jewish music in a 1920 cartoon on the pages of the Yiddish newspaper *The Jewish Daily Forward*: a cantor sings Aïda and a black man belts "Eli, Eli." The caption read, "An upside-down world."

But it wasn't. For Ethel Waters, the song spoke to a history of shared suffering. "It tells the tragic history of the Jews as much as one song can," she wrote in her autobiography, "and that history of their age-old grief and despair is so similar to that of my own people that I felt I was telling the story of my own race too." Then again, she also copped to having a good marketing strategy: "Jewish people in every town seemed to love the idea of me singing their song. They crowded the theaters to hear it, and they would tell one another: 'The *schwarze* sings "Eïli, Eïli"! The *schwarze*!'"

Al Jolson
The Jazz Singer
Sunbeam Records, 1974

George Jessel
The Last of the Minstrel Men
Design Records, 1959

Eddie Fisher
You Ain't Heard Nothin' Yet!
RCA Victor, 1968

George Gershwin
Rhapsody in Blue: An American in Paris
Wing, 1968

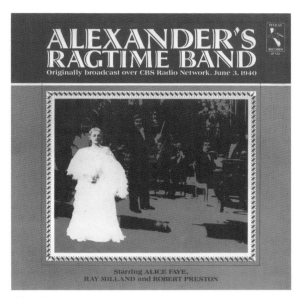

Original Cast
Alexander's Ragtime Band
Pelican, 1960s

Billy Eckstine and Sarah Vaughan
Billy Eckstine and Sarah Vauhan
Sing the Best of Irving Berlin
Mercury, 1957

Oscar Peterson
Oscar Peterson Plays the Harold Arlen Song Book
Verve, 1954

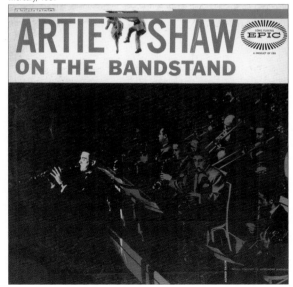

Artie Shaw
On the Bandstand
Epic, 1950s

That was Nat King Cole's rationale for doing "Nature Boy," a song penned by a Brooklyn Jew, born George Aberle, turned mystic vegetarian hippie eden ahbez. Ahbez, who renounced capital letters for his name, was a Jewish precursor to *Into the Wild*'s Chris McCandless, but instead of leaving the American East for an abandoned bus in Alaska, he ended up homesteading beneath the L of the Hollywood sign. For "Nature Boy," he lifted the melody from Herman Yablokoff's Yiddish song "Shvayg Mayn Harts" ("Be Still, My Heart") and Cole picked up on it—he wanted to do a song that would resonate with his Jewish audiences.

The rationale was more politically motivated for an artist like Paul Robeson. On his *Let Freedom Sing! Songs of Hope and Courage,* he includes "Zot Nit Keynmol" (Song of the Warsaw Ghetto). Or there was Johnny Mathis, who might be synonymous with chestnuts, open fires, and red cable-knit sweaters, but he's as earnest as he looks on the cover of *Good Night, Dear Lord* when he lends his hot-cocoa voice to "Eli, Eli," "Kol Nidre," and "Where Can I Go?" His decision to cover "Where Can I Go?" is a good reminder that a tune written in Yiddish about the Warsaw Ghetto took on a new life as a civil-rights anthem in the states, that "Where do I go?" has never been just a Jewish question.

One person who understood this notion well is David Axelrod, the son of Los Angeles Jewish lefties who grew up in South Central immersed in black music. His 1972 concept album dedicated to the history of black struggle, *The Auction,* which was coproduced by jazz legend Julian "Cannonball" Adderley, puts a slave market on its cover. It was a theme Axelrod started imagining four years earlier on *Release of an Oath* (an LP credited to the renowned psychedelic band the Electric Prunes that he wrote and arranged) where he turned the holiest of Jewish laments, "Kol Nidre," into a funk call to universal liberation against "the conqueror's yoke." Like so many other black and Jewish musicians, Axelrod tapped into the common ground of suffering and oppression, never forgetting that slavery and exile were black and Jewish themes alike.

But LPs didn't only celebrate this rosy side of the black-Jewish story. The ugly side was there too. It's hard to look at Al Jolson and Eddie Cantor's *The Immortals* without grappling with just how central blackface was to so many Jewish pop performers. Jolson's use of blackface helped him become a major national star, but that didn't stop him from being admired by African-American performers like Jackie Wilson, who pays tribute to Jolson on his *Nowstalgia* LP. On the cover, he's drenched in watercolors, a cover style that was

Willie "The Lion" Smith
Self-titled
Crescendo, 1972

Nat King Cole
Nature Boy
Capitol, 1965

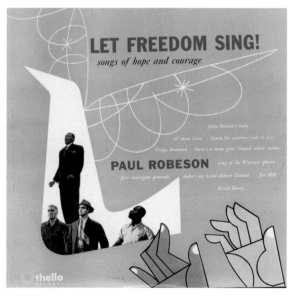

Paul Robeson
Let Freedom Sing! Songs of Hope and Courage
Othello, 1950s

WHAT IT SOUNDS LIKE

Diana Ross and the Supremes & the Temptations
On Broadway
Motown, 1969

Lamont Dozier on the Temptations' "Fiddler on the Roof Medley" from *On Broadway*

When I listen to the "Fiddler on the Roof Medley" by the Temptations, the thoughts that come to mind are that here we have a blend of two civil-rights minority groups coming together musically. The relationships between blacks and Jews are similar with regard to music, because of the social injustices both groups of people have suffered throughout the centuries. Their music reflects this, in the blues that the blacks sing and the messages found in the hymns and lyrical stories that the Jewish community have sung about and filmed and staged. Both groups are working through the music for civil rights, to keep it in the forefront of the minds of our people, so that we never forget the atrocities they faced, and so we are certain to make a better world for humanity. It also reminds people that Jews and blacks are not much different from any of us in our quests for a better life. At least that's the way I like to believe.

apparently quite popular. Nina Simone uses it on *Folksy Nina* (where the high priestess of political sixties soul does the Israeli showstopper "Erets Zavat Chalav") as does Eartha Kitt on *The Fabulous Eartha Kitt* (Kitt purrs and growls her way through two Hebrew school staples, "Sholem" and "Ki M'Tzion").

LPs by Jews in the world of jazz could fill a whole book of their own. Si Zentner leans on his trombone like he's posing for a Sears portrait, Fred Katz ends up in his pajamas on a Malibu beach serenading a blond Gidget, and Herbie Mann goes for the beefcake-flautist look, hoping we don't notice that he has more hair on his chest than he does on his head. The trumpeter Sonny Berman keeps it nice and simple on his 1946 album *Beautiful Jewish Music*. The liner notes resurrect an age-old claim: Jewish music, with its aches and cries, with its history of exile and migration and oppression, is the original black music: "Jewish cantors and gypsies sound more like it than anything from Africa."

Which means that on the cover, all we need is Sonny Berman. His white, round, chubby face is front and center, the Jew for whom black music is not a foreign language but allegedly, a native tongue.

Norman Granz
Jam Session
Verve, 1950s

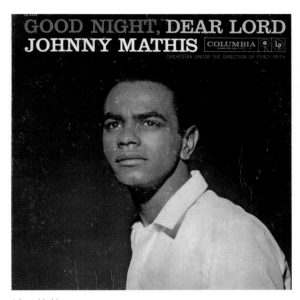

Johnny Mathis
Good Night, Dear Lord
Columbia, 1958

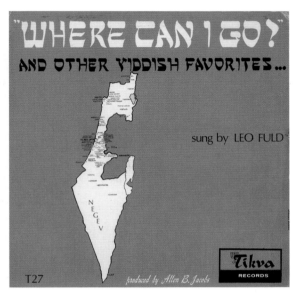

Leo Fuld
Where Can I Go? And Other Yiddish Favorites
Tikva, 1950s

Ray Charles
Ingredients in a Recipe for Soul
ABC Paramount, 1963

K & JJ
Israel
A&M, 1968

Eartha Kitt
The Fabulous Eartha Kitt
Kapp, 1959

Nina Simone
Folksy Nina
Colpix records, 1965

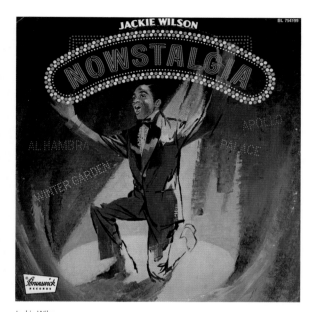

Jackie Wilson
Nowstalgia
Brunswick, 1974

Si Zentner and His Orchestra
A Thinking Man's Band
Liberty, 1959

Fred Katz
Fred Katz and His Jammers
Decca, 1958

Ziggy Elman and His Orchestra
Sentimental Trumpet
MGM, 1956

David A. Axelrod and Earl Palmer
The Auction
Decca, 1972

Oliver Wang on David Axelrod's *The Auction*

The one thing you could count on from David Axelrod at this point in his career was his unpredictability. Prior to *The Auction*, Axelrod had released one album based on the poems of William Blake, another as an environmental critique, and another that remakes Handel with Axelrod's baroque, beguiling mixtures of jazz, rock, and funk. With *The Auction*, Axelrod—collaborating with Cannonball Adderley—builds an entire concept album around American slavery. That point is brought home starkly on the title cut, as the slick, funky sound of Adderley's band gives way to the gravelly voice of Billie Barnum, who sings of "young girls...helpless in their shame" while soloist Gwendolyn Owens speaks of "little children sold...while masters traded them for gold." It's a heavy, bleak sentiment—oddly contrasted against Adderley's gliding grooves—but it's also the kind of eclectic and provocative work that Axelrod excelled at. Especially compared to the milquetoast soft-rock tunes and party-oriented funk slappers of the time, *The Auction* refuses to grant easy comfort.

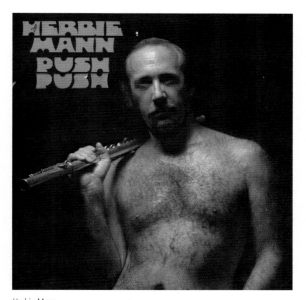

Herbie Mann
Push Push
Embryo, 1971

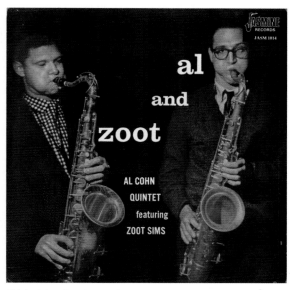

Al Cohn Quintet featuring Zoot Sims
Al and Zoot
Coral, 1958

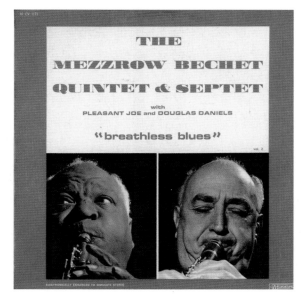

The Mezzrow Bechet Quintet & Septet
Breathless Blues
King Jazz, 1946

Sonny Berman
Beautiful Jewish Music
Onyx, 1973

WHO NEEDS A SYNAGOGUE WHEN YOU HAVE A RECORD PLAYER IN YOUR LIVING ROOM?: THE JEWISH HOLIDAYS AS LONG-PLAYING RECORDS

The Jewish people have never had to work too hard to develop a busy social calendar. Between the Sabbath and a never-ending panoply of festivals, their calendars feel like they are filled with more holidays than work days. And for every holiday there is a record. In contrast to the cantorial market, the primary audience for the majority of these disks was less the pious who lacked the patience to wait for the next festival and more those Jews whose ritual skills had become a little rusty but who wanted to pass a smattering of tradition on to the children anyway. This was vinyl in a new role—part storehouse of tradition, part educator, and part good excuse to just sit around and listen to the spinning record in lieu of leading the ritual themselves.

This was a contradictory time in terms of American Jewish observance. American Jews had just invented the great suburban synagogue—employing the finest wood, marble, and luxurious velvet. These vast complexes, with several sanctuaries, working kitchens, and in some cases swimming pools, were many things—status symbols, proclamations of empowerment, symbols of upward mobility, and social presence—but centers of spiritual community, not so much. Synagogue membership was high, but attendance had been in decline since the 1930s in face of stiff competition from

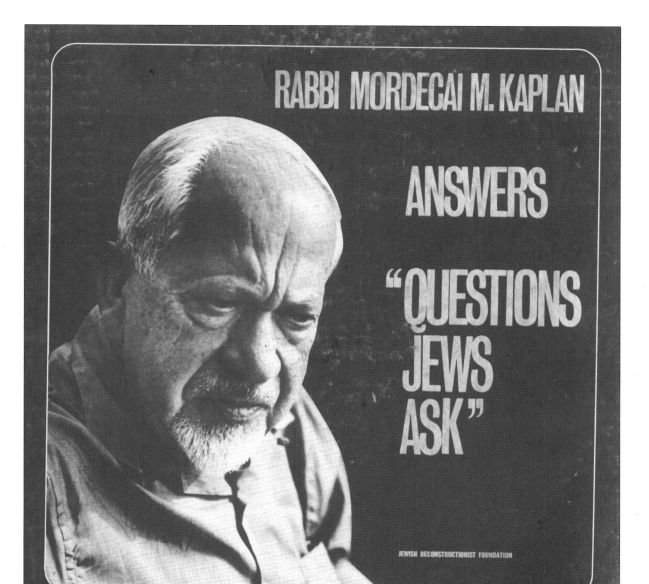

Mordecai M. Kaplan
Questions Jews Ask
Jewish Reconstructionist Records, 1963

Moishe Oysher
The Moishe Oysher Seder
Rozanna Records, c. 1940

Moishe Oysher
Kol Nidre Night with Moishe Oysher—1
Rozanna Records, c. 1940

Moishe Oysher
Kol Nidre Night with Moishe Oysher—2
Rozanna Records, c. 1940

Moishe Oysher
The Moishe Oysher Chanukah Party
Rozanna Records, c. 1940

the more universal venues, like cinema and musical theater. Jews loved jazz more than prayer. They built monumental synagogues, but they did not have to attend.

However, in the same period, an influx of Jewish thinkers to America in the wake of the Second World War catalyzed a revitalization of Judaism in this country, spearheaded by Mordecai Kaplan, Abraham Joshua Heschel, Emil Fackenheim, and Will Herberg. This intellectual movement led to a resurgence of interest in Jewish ideas, theology, and education. The serious thinking of the era was captured in the release of a six-album boxed set, *Rabbi Mordecai M. Kaplan Answers "Questions Jews Ask."* Kaplan, the pioneer of the Reconstructionist movement, which sought to adapt Hebraic tradition to modern American reality, graces the cover, modestly averting his gaze from the viewer while effortlessly dispatching over ninety questions posed by everyday Jews—from "How would you answer the question of a sick child who asks, 'Why did God make polio?'" to "Is there any warrant for the general apathy on the part of Jews to the fact that a large number among them are involved in all kinds of rackets and shady deals?"

The net effect was to usher in an era in which casual observance of some aspect of Judaism—lighting candles, Shabbat observance, and the Passover seder—increased even as daily religious practice and strict observance of Jewish laws, such as keeping kosher, declined. Most picked and chose what to follow and what not to, leading both to diversity and an emphasis on what was shared: language, culture, community, memory, and the major life-cycle holidays, which became, in the words of historian Jenna Weissman Joselit, "exuberant yet short-lived bursts of Judaism."

A barrage of Jewish holiday albums followed. Among the first to capitalize on the trend was the wonderfully named cantor and Yiddish film star, Moishe Oysher, who released a series of albums for the big three: Kol Nidre, Passover, and Chanukah. The albums, which all employ the same headshot of Oysher confidently staring down the assimilation that was seizing American Jews, feature his signature energetic singing, broken up by English narration and explanation by his sidekick, the slick-looking radio personality Barry Gray. The liner notes suggest that within Oysher's "blood [lies] the compressed yearnings of a long forgotten forbear." The Jewish market apparently agreed—these yearnings translated into impressive sales.

The arc of the Sabbath LP in particular illustrates the development on vinyl of American Jews' relationship to observance. As they became more American over time, their sense of what they wanted out of a religious experience evolved—English over Hebrew, a decrease in literal adherence to the texts, and a desire for the basics of Jewish education. These are all evident in the transition from albums like *Oneg Shabbat* and *Likrat Shabbat* to *The Joy of the Sabbath in Song and Story,* whose major selling point is that it is narrated in English. These albums became supplanted in the late sixties by disks that sought to transform the Sabbath itself to fit a more modern world. Artists like Moog pioneer Gershon Kingsley, the man who gave the world the formative electronica track "Popcorn," headed out to a synagogue in East Orange, New Jersey, to perform and, soon after, record *Shabbat for Today,* which sought to "Sing unto the Lord a new song." In similar fashion, *Hear, O Israel: A Concert Service in Jazz,* featuring the great Herbie Hancock on piano, has the holy scrolls hemmed in by trumpet, horn, and sax.

In terms of the holidays themselves, sociologist Marshall Sklare developed a rule of thumb as to which would be maintained and which discarded based on his 1950s ethnographic studies of Jews in a suburb of Chicago. Holidays that prospered had to meet a few prerequisites: They had to be capable of modern redefinition, they could not demand isolation from the rest of society, they had to coincide with a comparable universal holiday, they had to be child-centric, and possibly most important of all, they had to be infrequent. Simply put, if the holiday could survive beyond the synagogue and in the space of the home, with minimal ritual to get in the way of all the eating and kids' games, then it just might have a future.

Passover is the perfect example of how vinyl could squeeze celebration into the most American of formats while offering record companies a commercial opportunity. Rabbi Robert Kahn promises the listener "An American Home Service for the Passover" on *Your Seder,* the cover of which suggests an evening as stale as the bread of affliction it features. *Pesach* on Unbreakable Records illustrates what an American Home Service might look like—a nuclear family seated at the table with father startled by his son's ability to read the Haggadah while mother looks on adoringly. And to cap it all, opera star Richard Tucker seems stunned to discover that after going to the trouble of donning his cantorial garb, no one else has turned up at the seder.

The High Holy Day period—Rosh Hashanah and Yom Kippur—was another time of the year in which the ancestral call injected an adrena-

A. W. Binder
Jewish Holidays in Song
RCA Victor, c. 1940

Seymour Silbermintz
Jewish Children Sing with Seymour Silbermintz
Menorah Records, c. 1950

Hass Family Quartet
Songs of the Holidays and Festivals of All Year Round
Gila, 1960

Gladys Gewirtz; Eve Lippman; Sara G. Levy
Mother Goose Songs for Jewish Children and Holiday Play Songs
Menorah Records, c. 1950

Gershon Kingsley
Shabbat '68
Kingsley Sound, 1968

National Federation of Temple Youth
Hear, O Israel: A Concert Service in Jazz
Self-released, 1968

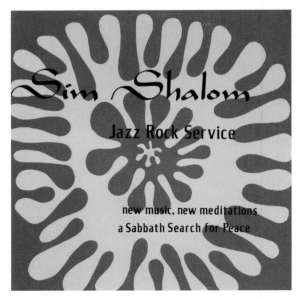

Gershon Kingsley
Shabbat for Today
Kingsley Sound, 1968

Sim Shalom
*Jazz Rock Service—New Music, New Meditations: A Sabbath
Search for Peace*
Queen City Album, 1970

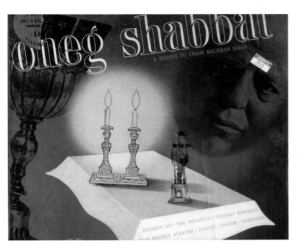

Various
Oneg Shabbat
Israel Music Productions, c. 1950

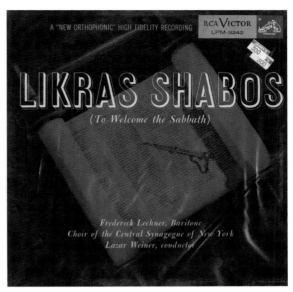

Lazar Weiner; Frederick Lechner
Likras Shabos
Famous Records, c. 1960

Chaim Yavin
The Joy of the Shabbath in Song and Story
CBS, c. 1970

Jason Bauch
A People That Sings—Lives!
Aleph, 1960s

lin shot of religious revitalization into even the nonobservant. In contrast to Passover, there was little about these festivals that could be rebranded as fun and exciting. The continued observance was more about muscle memory, and the somber tone of the covers of these holiday records reflects the ambience of awe and gravity that hangs over the synagogue aisles. Once again, the ever reliable Richard Tucker finds time to chip in with another classic cover, looking dumbfounded beside a floating shofar and prayer shawl.

The remaining Jewish festivals languished on vinyl as they did in real life. Despite the fact that Shavuot, Sukkoth, and, to a lesser extent, Purim were historically important, they did not make much of an impression as LPs. The one exception was Hanukkah, which had traditionally been a minor, arcane holiday. Its mixture of easy ritual, gift giving for the kids, malleable theme of freedom, and calendar potential for Christmas rivalry meant it had a secure spot in the Jewish year. But despite its popularity, it still paled in comparison to its jingle-bells counterpart, and the line between Hanukkah and Christmas soon began to blur. Albums like *Chanukah Carols* and *Have a Jewish Christmas...?* acted like gateway drugs, leading irresistibly to living rooms adorned with the euphemistic flora of the "Hanukkah bush" and albums like Barbra Streisand's *A Christmas Album,* in which Yentl herself was cloaked in Christmas glow, reminding us more than ever that Jesus was once just a Jewish carpenter.

Isaac C. Avigdor
The Voice of the Seder
Unknown, 1950s

Arthur Asher, A. J. Kalb, Eve Lippman
Pesach
Menorah Records, c. 1960

Malavsky Family
The Passover Festival
Tikva, c. 1959

Robert I. Kahn
*Your Seder: An American Home
Service for the Passover*
El Al Records, 1960

Richard Tucker
A Passover Seder Festival
Columbia, 1953

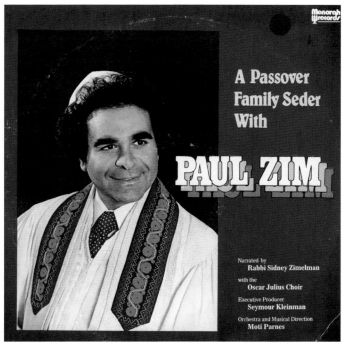

Paul Zim
*A Passover Family Seder
with Paul Zim*
Menorah Records, 1979

Abraham Behrman; Richard J. Neumann; Murray Lane
Closing Service Yom Kippur
Collectors Guild, 1961

Paul Zim
The Liturgy in Song for the New Year
Menorah Records, 1980

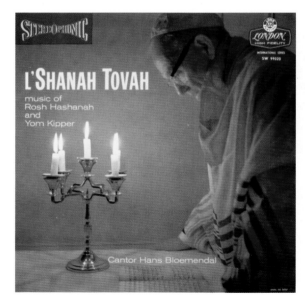

Hans Bloemendal
L'Shanah Tovah
London Records, c. 1969

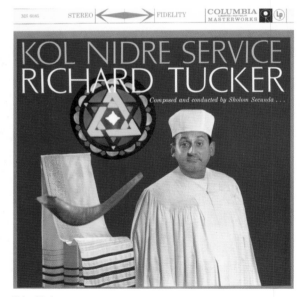

Richard Tucker
Kol Nidre Service
Columbia, 1959

Sol Zim
The Joy of Chanukah
Zimray, 1979

Gefilte Joe and the Fish
Hanukkah Rocks
Rhino, 1978

Stanley Adams; Chicken Flickers
Chanukah Carols
Sight and Sound, c. 1960

Ray Brenner; Len Weinrib; Barry E. Blitzer
Have a Jewish Christmas . . . ?
Tower, 1967

Barbra Streisand
A Christmas Album
Columbia, 1967

CHAPTER FIVE

ME LLAMO STEINBERG:
THE JEWISH LATIN CRAZE

One of the greatest testaments to the flexibility of Jewish tradition is also probably one of the least talked about: the Jewish Latin craze of the 1950s.

Only two years after the first LPs were commercially introduced in 1948, all of America was delirious with Mambo Mania. Thanks to the music and dance moves of Cuban bandleader Pérez Prado, fifties America had become Mambo USA. Arthur Murray was teaching his former fox trot students to mambo, dance halls from New York to L.A. were hosting packed mambo nights, *The Jackie Gleason Show* kept mambo bands on national TV, mambo rhythms and dance sequences popped up in Hollywood musicals, and a marquee mambo concert tour brought artists like Machito and Joe Loco to cities across the country.

American Jews were the mambo craze's earliest adopters, earning their own Yiddish-inflected moniker—the mamboniks. Jews had lived alongside Latinos in the Bronx, Brooklyn, and Harlem, and Yiddish radio shows often shared the same frequencies as Latin music programs, so it wasn't surprising that even before the LP came around, Jews had already been reliable supporters of Latin music. The great early pop stylist Irving Kaufman had already unleashed "Moe the Schmo Takes a Rhumba Lesson," bawdy balladeer Ruth Wallis had already declared "It's a Scream How Levine Does the Rhumba," and Yiddish comic Willie Howard had already put on a sombrero

BAGELS and BONGOS

IRVING FIELDS TRIO

HI FI
DECCA
RECORDS

including:
WHERE SHALL I GO · RAISINS AND ALMONDS · BELZ
MY YIDDISHE MOMME · BEI MIR BIST DU SCHÖN

Irving Fields Trio
Bagels and Bongos
Decca, 1959

Sy Menchin and His Steven Scott Orchestra
My Bubba & Zaeda's Cha Cha Cha
Apollo, 1959

Irving Fields Trio
More Bagels and Bongos
Decca, 1960

to become Tyrone Shapiro, the Bronx Caballero, in the 1935 film *Rose of the Rancho.*

By the time the mambo and the *cha-cha-cha* hit big in the fifties—when the whole country was, as Mickey Katz sang on "Yiddishe Mambo," on a Latin kick—Latin music was becoming the preferred soundtrack to Jewish-American leisure time. Max Hyman, the Jewish owner of the famed New York City nightclub the Palladium, instituted an all-Latin music policy in 1949, and there was no stopping the influence of artists like Tito Rodriguez and Tito Puente on the Jewish musical imagination. Jewish recreational centers and synagogues hosted Latin dance parties, and soon no bar mitzvah was complete without a mambo interlude. If you believe Sy Menchin and His Steven Scott Orchestra (Steven and Scott were Sy's sons), even the seniors crowd of dancing *bubbas* and *zaydas* couldn't resist the temptation of "Yossel, Yossel" done as a cha-cha.

As the headquarters of Jewish leisure, the hotels of the Catskills mountains and their "Borscht Belt" entertainment circuit became key laboratories of the Jewish-Latin mash-up. Catskills entertainment scouts were among the first U.S. promoters to book acts from Cuba and Puerto Rico, and Catskills ballrooms became indispensable venues for top Latin dance bands and handsome dance instructors.

Everyone came through Sullivan County, New York, from ballroom mainstays like Cuban bandleader Emilio Reyes to legends in the making like Puerto Rican pianist Eddie Palmieri and Latin Jazz visionary Machito (who even put out his own tribute to the Catskills entertainment landscape, *Vacation at the Concord*).

Remember, when nobody was allowed "to put Baby in the corner" in *Dirty Dancing,* she was a Jewish girl learning to dance the mambo.

Puerto Rican pianist Johnny Conquet memorialized the Catskills scene on his 1958 album, *Raisins & Almonds Cha Cha Cha & Merengues*—a studio recording masquerading as a live Catskills show in the "Cha Cha Chateau" of the make-believe "Merengue Manor" resort. The album's liner notes even copy the format of a Catskills hotel newsletter (in the style of Grossinger's daily *Tattler*) called the "Nosherei News." Conquet performs a mostly Jewish-based musical repertoire— "Freilach Merengue," "Sher Cha Cha," "Matzoh Ball Merengue," and a merengue version of "Roumania, Roumania"—but also provides a glossary that translates the album's Yiddish phrases into English for those "who want to be with it when you land in cha cha territory."

The ultimate Latin Catskills album, though,

belongs to Puerto Rican percussion king Tito Puente, who released *Cha Cha with Tito Puente at Grossinger's* in 1959. On the cover, designed by *Mad* magazine legend Jack Davis, Puente looks as happy as can be, pounding the timbales in a ketchup-red dinner jacket and honey-mustard-yellow bow tie. Puente rips through familiar favorites like "Baubles, Bangles, and Beads" and "How High the Moon" but also does "Mañana Nicaragua" and "Miami Beach Rumba," two compositions by the less familiar Campos El Pianista, better known by his Jewish nom de piano, Irving "Fabulous Fingers" Fields.

Irving Fields did Yiddish theater, symphonic jazz, and cruise ships before giving in to the Latin bug and turning the pop standard "Autumn Leaves" into "Miami Beach Rhumba," a song that would be covered by everyone from Yiddish singer Seymour Rechtzeit to the popular Latin society band Pancho and His Orchestra before exploding as a commercial hit for Spanish bandleader Xavier Cugat. The same year Puente thrilled audiences at Grossinger's, Fields released *Bagels and Bongos,* a collection of Yiddish favorites reimagined in Latin arrangements. We like to think of it as the *White Album* of the Jewish Latin craze.

This LP was the perfect snapshot of American Jewish taste at the midcentury mark, fusing the Jewish songbook that audiences were slowly leaving behind (yet still emotionally connected to) with the new-fangled Latin rhythms they were embracing with unprecedented zeal (so much so that *More Bagels and Bongos* would follow soon after). *Bagels and Bongos* was a smash with Jewish audiences, and its cover—an elegant still life of frozen dance and drum—is the minimalist masterpiece of the Latin-Jewish glory days that it helped ignite.

In our search for LP evidence of the Jewish Latin craze, though, we quickly found that it wasn't just Jews dancing and playing Latin music, but Latino artists themselves who were taking a swing at Jewish musical favorites. Cuban bandleader Pérez Prado turned "Hava Nagila" into a mambofied twist on his *Twist Goes Latin!* album, Machito did a whole LP of Irving Berlin standards, the Ames Brothers joined forces with visionary Mexican composer Juan García Esquivel on their *Hello, Amigos* LP, and Joe Quijano showed us what happens when, inevitably, *Fiddler on the Roof Goes Latin.* And we can't forget Eydie Gormé, who may be best known as the Vegas sidekick of her Jewish hubby Steve Lawrence, but was born Edith Gormezano to Sephardic Spanish parents in the Bronx. On her first solo album,

Tito Rodriguez
Tito Rodriguez at the Palladium
United Artists, 1960

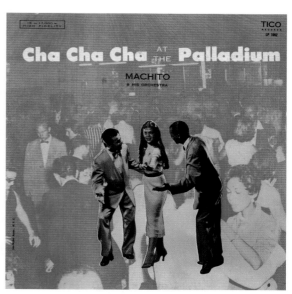

Machito
Cha Cha Cha at the Palladium
Tico, 1959

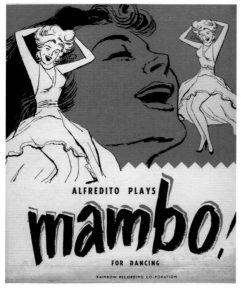

Alrefito
Alfredito Plays Mambo! for Dancing
Rainbow, 1950s

Pupi Campo
12 Cha-Chas and Merengues
Hollywood, 1956

Juan Calle and His Latin Lantzmen
Mazel Tov, Mis Amigos
Riverside, 1961

Wil-Dog Abers of Ozomatli on Juan Calle and His Latin Lanzmen's *Mazel Tov, Mis Amigos*

Their "O Momme!" sounds like Puerto Ricans in a *comparsa* (conga band) parade that turns into a Jewish wedding march, then during the solos you find yourself ballroom dancing to the baddest musicians of the time. I love how the cuatro (Puerto Rican guitar) and flute have to share the same solo. Either the band leader didn't like them or there wasn't enough time on the track to fit them both in. It sounds like a huge struggle over who got to take the lead. When I heard their "Freilach a Nacht," my first instinct was to loop the opening drums and write a song off them. Then after the piano intro, they break into a merengue. It is dope!!! All I can say is, I can't bow down enough for Charlie Palmieri. He is the greatest of all time.

she looks like a matinee sweetheart lost in a bamboo grove, innocent as to what would lie ahead: a string of collaborations with the classic Mexican trio Los Panchos that would make her a household name in the Spanish-speaking world.

The Jewish love of Latin music also left its mark on some of the most influential Latin record labels. Sidney Siegel ran the pioneering Seeco Records, a label he dedicated to "the finest in Latin-American recordings." Al Santiago founded Alegre Records in 1955 with the financial support of Jewish businessman Ben Perlman (the owner of Grossman's Clothes, the business next to Santiago's record store). And Tico Records was the joint venture of Art Raymond, a legndary Yiddish music radio DJ, and George Goldner, a ragman turned music man with a Puerto Rican wife. Their first major hit, Tito Puente's "Albaniquito," featured the legendary likes of Mario Bauzá, Mongo Santamaría, and Vicentico Valdes.

The mambo craze may have faded by the 1960s, but plenty of Jews stayed involved in the now growing salsa scene. Among the most famous is Larry Harlow, who started his life as Ira Kahn in Brooklyn, went to study music in Havana, and came back as El Judío Maravilloso, the Marvelous Jew, the pianist and leader of Orchestra Harlow. He's been involved in over two hundred salsa recordings with powerhouse label Fania Records, including the early *El Exigente* (The Demanding One). As salsa legend Jimmy Sabater has said of Harlow, "That guy's Puerto Rican! He ain't Jewish. He walks, talks, eats, sleeps, drinks Puerto Rican. He's *mishpucha* [family]." Harlow gave vibraphone lessons to another respected Jewish salsero, Harvey Averne, who began his career as Arvito before owning up to his birthright as the leader of both the Harvey Averne Dozen and the Harvey Averne Barrio Band.

As central as New York was to the Jewish-Latin boom, the LPs remind us that the West Coast was in on it too. Mexican-American pianist and Los Angeles native Eddie Cano makes "Hava Nagila" part of the "lusty Latin stylings" of his *Mucho Piano!* album, and on the cover of the 1972 debut by California Chicano funk legends Azteca is a rock-and-roll Aztec calendar (note the piano keys and electric guitars) like none ever found in Tenochtitlán. It's credited to the great Aztec artist billed only as "Steinberg"—beloved *New Yorker* cover artist Saul Steinberg.

The West Coast also gave us Rene Bloch. Born to French Jews who immigrated to Sonora, Mexico, before they moved the family

Leon Kelner and His Orchestra
Cha Cha Cha Anyone?
MGM, 1957

Johnny Conquet, His Piano & Orchestra
Raisins & Almonds Cha Cha Cha & Merengues
RCA Victor, 1958

Sonny Rossi and the Concord Hotel Orchestra
Cha Cha Cha at the Concord
Mardi Gras Records, 1960s

Emilio Reyes and His Orchestra
Perfect Dance Tempos for Latin Lovers
Decca, 1960

Tito Puente
Cha Cha with Tito Puente at Grossinger's
RCA Victor, 1960

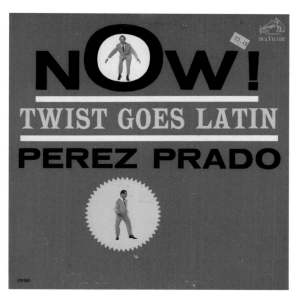

Perez Prado
Now! Twist Goes Latin
RCA Victor, 1962

The Ames Brothers
Hello Amigos
RCA Victor, 1960

Machito
Mi Amigo, Machito
Forum, 1959

north to Los Angeles, Bloch became a primo sax man in the L.A. R & B scene, dropping one of the quintessential West Coast jazz solos when he gigged with the Johnny Otis Band on 1945's "Harlem Nocturne." Bloch set out on his own in the fifties and led a number of different Latin dance bands that partnered with big-name East Coast players like Tito Puente, Mongo Santamaría, and Pérez Prado.

Better known is the story of Herb Alpert, undoubtedly the most famous Jewish musician to go Latin of all time. His numerous albums of perky brass and lulling marimbas with the half-Jewish, half-Italian Tijuana Brass made him one of the top four album-selling artists of the sixties (he was in distinguished company alongside the Beatles, Elvis, and Frank Sinatra). Alpert spawned plenty of copycats, chief among them another Jewish musician with a taste for virtual south-of-the-border sounds, Alpert's marimba specialist Julius Wechter. Wechter's Baja Marimba Band turn Jewish-Mexican musical exchange into an interethnic gag, posing in floppy sombreros, goofy bandito mustaches, and mariachi–meets–Wild West costumes. Another of Alpert's fellow travelers was Jose Jimenez, the bumbling Mexican immigrant infamously played by comedian Bill Dana on *The Steve Allan Show*, *The Bill Dana Show*, and on a slew of LPs.

Mambo Mania may have fizzled by the end of the fifties, and the Tijuana Brass boom may have run out of steam by the end of the sixties, but comedian Lou Jacobi still managed to make fun of both flare-ups of Jewish Latinophilia on his 1966 LP *Al Tijuana and His Jewish Brass*, where he dons a bullfighter outfit and walks through the streets of the Lower East Side surrounded by African-American and Latino kids.

"This is Al Tijuana and my Jewish Brass," Jacobi announces, "Pedro, Manuel, Pablo, José, Miguel, Ricardo, Juan, and . . . Sheldon."

Eydie Gormé
Self-titled
Coral, 1957

Various
Seeco Sampler of Latin Rhythms
Seeco, late 1950s

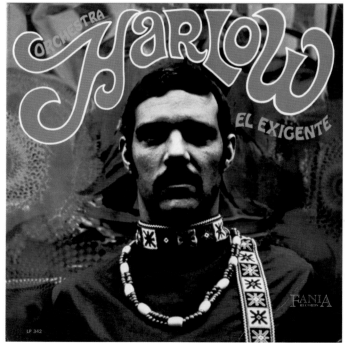

Orchestra Harlow
El Exigente
Fania, 1967

Orchestra Harlow
Hommy: A Latin Opera
Fania, 1973

Orchestra Harlow
El Judio Maravilloso
Fania, 1975

The Harvey Averne Dozen
Viva Soul
Atlantic, 1968

Azteca
Self-titled
Columbia, 1972

Eddie Cano
Mucho Piano: The Lusty Latin Stylings of Eddie Cano
GNP, 1962

Rene Bloch and Orchestra
Mucho Rock
VSOP, 1958

Herb Alpert & the Tijuana Brass
The Lonely Bull
A&M, 1962

Baja Marimba Band
Self-titled
A&M, 1965

Herb Alpert & the Tijuana Brass
South of the Border
A&M, 1963

Yeshiva Brass
Self-titled
Fran Record Co., 1969

Bob Booker & George Foster
present
Al Tijuana and his Jewish Brass

Al Tijuana and His Jewish Brass
Bob Booker & George Foster Present Al Tijuana and His Jewish Brass
Capitol, 1966

Bill Dana
Jose Jimenez in Orbit/ Bill Dana on Earth
Kapp, 1960

Bill Dana
My Name . . . Jose Jimenez
Signature, 1959

CHAPTER SIX

LAUGHING AT 33 RPM:

THE VINYL WORLD OF COMEDY

When we began digging for all this Jewish gold, there were moments when it seemed as if comedy albums might have been the only albums Jews ever made. We know the LP was not invented to record Jews cracking jokes, but judging by the sheer surplus of the stuff, it sure started to feel that way.

So we checked around and found that in 1970, the psychologist Samuel Janus wagered that nearly 80 percent of the top comedians in the country were Jewish. "To most Americans," Janus mused, "comic and Jew are synonymous." He studied seventy-six different Jewish comics, subjecting each to three-hour clinical interviews, and found that most located the roots of comedy in a life spent in poverty and despair and equated "poverty and despair as a condition of being Jewish in a Gentile world." The abundance of LPs we found was evidence of a Jewish formula in the making: To be a comic is to be Jewish is to be poor and in despair.

The cover of Rodney Dangerfield's first album, *The Loser,* would have been a perfect companion to the Janus study. Here's the comic Jew (born Jacob Cohen, working as Jack Roy before becoming Rodney Dangerfield) stranded by the side of the road in the middle of Manhattan, his car broken down and teetering on a jack, reduced to flagging down help that never comes. Rodney was born in a holy suburb—Babylon, Long Island—but was now reduced to being a common urban victim, expelled from the land of the Hanging Gardens and Jones Beach to suffer alone in traffic. Even lifting his alias from *The Adventures of Ozzie and Harriet* ("Rodney Dangerfield" had been used by Jack Benny

Belle Barth
The Customer Comes First
Lobo, 1960s

WHY JEWS LAUGH

Rabbi Philip S. Bernstein

On the evening of June 30th, 1970, in the courtyard of his beloved Temple B'rith Kodesh in Rochester, New York, Rabbi Philip S. Bernstein regaled a thousand willing victims with a hilarious lecture on "Why Jews Laugh." "Why not?" asked Rabbi Bernstein.

The birds twittered over the Sukkah frame; the wind whistled through the microphone; the audience guffawed uncontrollably; all this is in the ambience of the happy occasion.

Humor for relief, humor for balance, humor for insight, and humor just for fun, are all aptly illustrated in this joyous record.

Rabbi Bernstein, B.A., M.H.L., D.D., D.S.Th., has the gift of laughter. Come share it with him.

Philip Sidney Bernstein
Why Jews Laugh
Mitch Miller, 1970

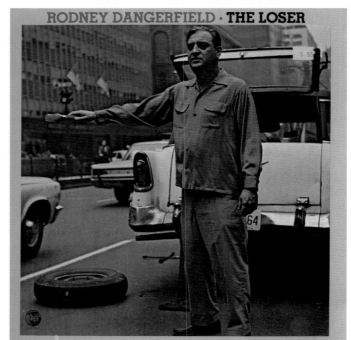

Rodney Dangerfield
The Loser
Rhino, 1978

but then became teen idol Ricky Nelson's nickname) couldn't rescue him from Loserville.

Lawrence Epstein has written of Jewish comics as "emotional pioneers" lighting out for the uncharted territory, "guides to the new frontiers of American life." In the sixties, that tangle with white-picket-fence Americanism was at a fever pitch as Jews sought out Babylon to become suburban Everypeople. As most histories spin it, the story of Jewish stand-up is the story of the Jewish suburbs, the story of Jews emerging from the anti-Semitic fog of the twenties, thirties, and forties, cashing in on the GI Bill, and heading out into the suburban sunshine of American prosperity. The LPs born alongside the suburban boom follow Jewish comedy from Catskills *tummling* in the Concord dining room to stand-up ranting at smoke-choked nightclubs, from ethnicity-drenched Yiddish theaters and vaudeville halls to the ethnically flavored Broadway stage. In the fifties, a former vaudevillian like Milton Berle could become TV's first true national star, and a former Catskills joker like Phil "The King of Chutzpah" Silvers could make the whole country laugh starring as an Army clown in *Sgt. Bilko*.

But the real milestone arrived with Shelley Berman, sitting on a stool dressed in a handsome suit with a cigarette in one hand and an imaginary phone in the other. His 1959 album *Inside Shelley Berman* was the first solo comedy LP to go gold and become a major national hit, hanging out in the *Billboard* Top 40 for two and a half years. Decades before Berman would play Larry David's dad on *Curb Your Enthusiasm*, he was a midcentury phenomenon, and the first sign that the LP could predict the Jewish future. After *Inside Shelley Berman* came the sixties, the official decade of Jewish universalism. Once the sixties were in full swing, the whole country already knew Anne Frank's diary by heart, had already seen Eichmann pay for his sins on TV, already started dreaming of a shtetl vacation thanks to *Fiddler on the Roof*, and as far as actual Jews themselves were concerned, the Six-Day War helped give them extra security by proxy—safe abroad, beloved at home. As Leslie Fielder quipped, Zion was now Main Street.

The comedic manifesto for this new era was *You Don't Have to Be Jewish*, an LP of studio-staged comedy sketches and an apt slogan for the glory days of Jewish comedy albums. "You don't have to be Jewish to enjoy this album," the back cover announces. "Here is contemporary humor and the classic comic philosophy that transcends national origin, family background, and cultural heritage. Laughter is ageless and international." The proof was in the production. The cast might have had some you-do-have-to-be-Jewish heavy hitters like Lou Jacobi and Betty Walker (best known as Molly

Goldberg's neighbor on *The Goldbergs*), but the album's creators, Bob Booker and George Foster, were actual Gentiles, not Jews with new last names. They had a hit with their 1962 JFK goof, *The New First Family,* but it was the Jewish franchise that brought the most success, spawning two follow-ups: one that gave anybody the chance to be Jewish (*When You're in Love the Whole World Is Jewish*) and one that worried that maybe too many were opting in (*The Yiddish Are Coming! The Yiddish Are Coming!*).

The Jewish move to the suburbs and into the American mainstream proved fertile ground for Allan Sherman, a TV producer turned song parodist who become a country-wide pop sensation with his 1962 debut *My Son, the Folk Singer.* The cover was as good an illustration as any of how much the Jewish role in American life had changed—Sherman sings atop a Roman pedestal with the symbols of his Jewishness down below: a seltzer bottle, a sliced loaf of rye, a hanging salami, and a bagel that has been tossed on the floor.

Sherman then went on to sing songs about middle-class Jews like "Harvey and Sheila," who bought a house with a pool and traded JFK for the GOP. His bit had so much traction that it spawned several imitations: Stan Ross's mother introduced his Shermanesque batch of songs as *My Son the Copy Cat* and Sam Chalpin's son traded his mother for his father

on *My Father the Pop Singer* (it was a painful joke on Dad, an immigrant cantor who was made to play the shlumping greenhorn naïf on the cover and then struggle through rushed renditions of "Leader of the Pack" and "I Want to Hold Your Hand").

Yet the more we collected, the more we realized that these tales of suburbia and Jewish universalism weren't the only ones out there. Plenty of old-timers used the LP to keep their older material alive as well. Henny Youngman's violin barrage of one-liners got even more extended runs with the LP. The Barton Brothers, who got their big break before the war turning a Yiddish radio commercial for a tailor into a millions-selling Yinglish pop hit ("Joe and Paul"), tried to keep the old shtick alive on *Stories Our Jewish Mother Forgot to Tell Us.*

Myron Cohen wasn't reviving old material, he was an actual throwback, specializing in quaint tales of nose jobs and matzo-ball soup that went over well on the senior circuit in the 1960s, where nostalgia and such in-group gags still killed.

In other words, Cohen was the anti–Lenny Bruce. Bruce might have dabbled in Yiddish accents early on and surely drew from the dysfunctional well of Jewish home life, but he quickly emerged as the Beat era's premier Jewish jazz voice; instead of looking back like Cohen, Bruce stayed dangerously and painfully

Milton Berle
Songs My Mother Loved
Roulette, 1957

John Philip Sousa and Edwin Franko Goldman
Bilko Marches
Promenade, 1958

Shelley Berman
Inside Shelley Berman
Verve, 1959

Pearl Willams
*Bagels &
Lox!*
Laff, 1960s

Sandra Bernhard on Pearl Williams's *Bagels and Lox*

Just when she finished her shtick, it segued right into Donna Summers singing "Bad Girls," and she sounded like Lenny Bruce lite, another great Jewish broad cutting through the bullshit.

current. Cohen was Miami Beach. Bruce was Greenwich Village, jail cells, and courtrooms. His *Interviews of Our Times* was just one example of how he traded schmaltz for brainy social commentary and religious critique—a move that Mort Sahl would pick up and run with on LPs like *The Next President*—but he was gone in a cloud of cops, drugs, and obscenity laws by 1966, the first casualty of Jewish comedy going so far out that there was no turning back.

Bruce once opened for Belle "I'm the kind of gal who wouldn't hurt a fly unless it was open" Barth, one of the prime denizens of a world that flourished on LP and has now been mostly forgotten. Hers was the heyday of a bawdy, raspy-voiced crew of Jewish female comics who only played blue, mixed Yiddish and English, and chased cigarettes with martinis. Barth got her start in the Catskills in the thirties but was the queen of the adults-only lady comics of the fifties and sixties, a trash-talking crew who bridged the gap between Fanny Brice and Joan Rivers, and included Pearl Williams, Rusty Warren, Patsy Abbot, and Ruth Wallis.

Pearl Williams wore mink shawls and spilled out of her dresses on the cover of nine LPs, and Ruth Wallis became the Jewish Redd Foxx, releasing LP after LP of risqué material—her *Here's Looking up Your Hatch* was one of eight potty-mouthed albums for Cincinnati's King label. Totie Fields was never as dirty as the blue comics (and as a result was far more beloved and accepted by the entertainment mainstream), but like them she made comedy about and through her body. On the cover of her only LP, *Totie Fields Live*, she made her shape into her subject and she looked, as she would say in the opening minutes of her show, "adoooorable."

Of all the Jewish comics, though, few took advantage of the medium as a platform for visual expression quite like Mickey Katz. The Yinglish-twisting musical comedian and parodist made every LP count. He dressed up as a cigar-smoking Jewish court jester, a cigar-smoking baby boy about to have his bris, a Mitch Miller look-alike, a UN delegate from Delancey Street, a meshuga rock and roller, a high society tux-and-tails sophisticate, and perhaps most famous of all, a deli worker from Canter's Deli on Fairfax in L.A., propped up on a butcher's block surrounded by hanging meats and clutching his trusty clarinet. Katz often got into trouble for his hyper-Jewish parodies of pop songs, and the LP covers just made it worse. There was no denying it. This was not *Hello, Dolly*. This was *Hello, Solly*.

Coming upon the Katz LPs was a worthy reminder that these album covers are not simply windows into the transitions of Jewish life in the 1950s and '60s. Sometimes they could also be audacious cultural prods, as effective and radical then as they are now.

Benny Fields, Jack Benny, Milton Berle, George Burns, Phil Silvers
Benny Fields and His Minstrel Men
Colpix, c. 1965

Bob Booker, George Foster
You Don't Have to Be Jewish
Kapp, 1965

Bob Booker, George Foster, Frank Gallp, Lou Jacobi
When You're in Love the Whole World Is Jewish
Kapp, 1966

Sol Weinstein, Frank Peppiatt, John Aylesworth, Dick Williams, Lou Jacobi
The Yiddish Are Coming! The Yiddish Are Coming!
Verve, 1967

Art Baer, Al Kelly, Minerva Pious, Larry Albert, Rhoda Brown, Rhoda Mann
Funny, You Don't Look It
RCA Victor, 1966

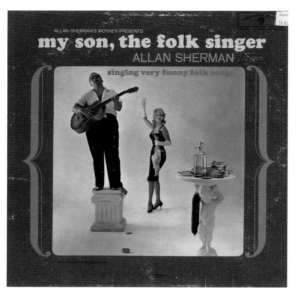

Allan Sherman
My Son, the Folk Singer
Warner Bros., 1962

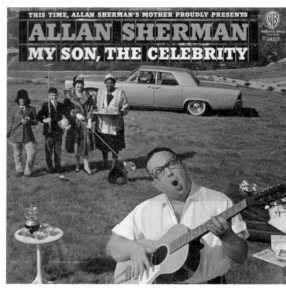

Allan Sherman
My Son, the Celebrity
Warner Bros., 1963

Stan Ross
My Son the Copy Cat
Del-fi, 1963

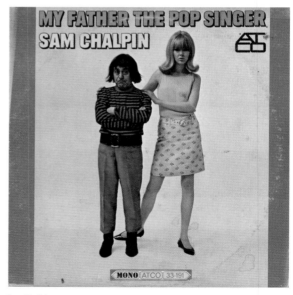

Sam Chalpin
My Father the Pop Singer
Atco, 1966

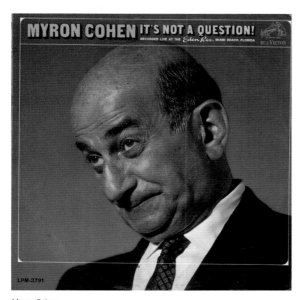

Myron Cohen
It's Not a Question!
RCA, 1967

Lenny Bruce
Lenny Bruce's Interviews of Our Times
Fantasy, 1959

Mort Sahl
The Next President
Verve, 1960

Jackie Mason
I'm the Greatest Comedian in the World
Only Nobody Knows It Yet
Verve, 1962

Various
The Great Tradition
Independent release, 1975

The Barton Brothers
Stories Our Jewish Mother
Forgot to Tell Us
Jubilee, 1966

Pearl Williams
A Trip Around the World Is Not a Cruise
After Hours, 1962

Belle Barth
My Next Story Is a Little Risqué
After Hours, 1962

Sophie Tucker
Bigger and Better Than Ever
Mercury, 1957

WHAT IT SOUNDS LIKE

Aimee Bender on Sophie Tucker's *Bigger and Better Than Ever*

At first, Sophie Tucker just made me angry. She speaks to the audience in rhyming, nicely paced monologues. Her voice has that pleasant smoker's edge to it, the voice of a dame, voices we don't hear so much anymore. She called herself "The Last of the Red Hot Mamas," and there's an appealing combination of toughness and womanliness and saucy sexuality to everything she says. But, whew! The advice! It's difficult to imagine, these days: a smoky bar, with a woman up at the front, dressed in feathers, telling everyone to be smiling all the time. Something complex is being given to the audience: a presentation of an American ideal, a bootstrapping self-improver, an uber-woman who cares, but beneath it she doesn't allow a lot of room for a listener to interpret, or muse, so there is also an asking, of the listeners, to hand over personal responsibility to Sophie, who knows what's best. I was driving around L.A. listening to her, and all of it was making me feel very relieved that I was born after feminism.

But on further listenings, I softened to her quite a bit. When she's freely talking about her sexual appetite, her voice carries a great va-va-va-voom flirtation, taunting the audience. Much of this feels playful, and I'm sure it was notably edgy at the time, but a severe loneliness comes through as well, because it seems as if she is trying to convince me of something, that she is also pushing to sell herself as the liberated insatiable woman. By the end songs, she is even saying that maybe men from outer space will be able to handle her better, as no human seems to be up for it, and there's a bit of later Judy Garland in her here, in the big-eyed, low-voiced combination of simmering anger and powerful yearning.

What did she represent? The new Jew in the new world, empowered? A semitic Mae West? Walking on the streets of gold, but soaked in pain beneath? Trying so hard to put the past behind, yet also drowning in it?

Belle Barth and Pearl Williams
Belle Barth Vs. Pearl Williams: Return Battle of the Mothers
Riot, 1960s

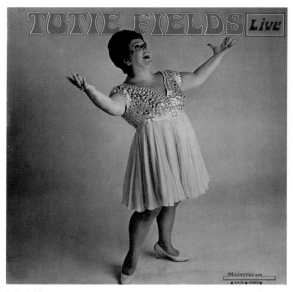

Totie Fields
Totie Fields Live
Mainstream, 1969

Ruth Wallis
The Admiral's Daughter Sez Here's Looking Up Your Hatch
King, 1966

Rusty Warren
Knockers Up!
Jubilee, 1960

Patsy Abbott
Have I Had You Before
Chess, 1961

Bob Booker, George Foster
The Jewish American Princess
Bell, 1971

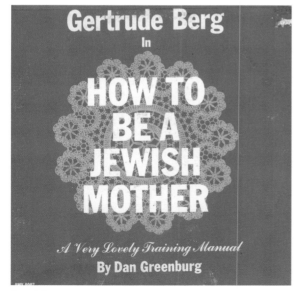

Gertrude Berg
How to Be a Jewish Mother
AMY, 1964

Harvey Jacobs, D.J. Martin, Victor Goldring
Mrs. Portnoy's Retort
United Artists, 1969

Max Asnas

CORNED-BEEF CONFUCIUS

RECORDED LIVE AT THE
STAGE DELICATESSEN
IN NEW YORK

Featuring
SHOW BIZ GREATS
in a riot of impromptu gag-sessions with Max Asnas, The Corned-Beef Confucius

KIMBERLY 2006

Design/Photography: Studio Five

Max Asnas
Corned-Beef Confucius
Kimberly, 1950s

Marty Allen and Steve Rossi
Batman & Rubin
Mercury, 1967

Larry Best
Color Me Jewish
Rivoli, 1950s

Mickey Katz
Mish Mosh
Capitol, 1957

Mickey Katz
Sing-Along with Mickele
Capitol, 1962

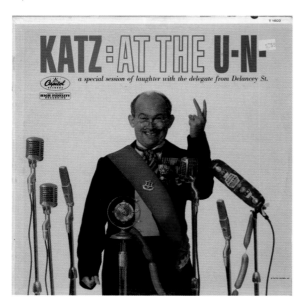

Mickey Katz
Katz: At the U.N.
Capitol, 1961

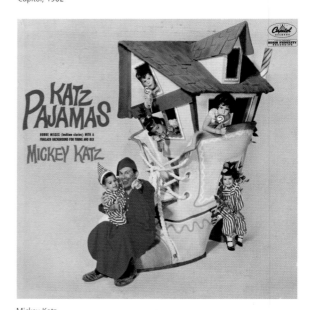

Mickey Katz
Katz Pajamas
Capitol, 1959

Mickey Katz
The Most Mishige: Mickey Katz
Capitol, 1958

Mickey Katz
Mickey Katz: The Borscht Jester
Capitol, 1960

Mickey Katz
Borscht by Mickey Katz
RCA Victor, 1954

Mickey Katz
Comin' 'Round the Katzkills
Capitol, 1960

CHAPTER SEVEN

"OH WHAT A NIGHT!": PARTIES, WEDDINGS, LOVE, AND GOOD OLD-FASHIONED HAPPINESS

We would wager that few albums have been the soundtrack to more heated arguments than these gems. Here is a collection cut to celebrate the times when Jewish families come together and celebrate, be it for a wedding, bar mitzvah, or just a party for party's sake. By the 1950s vinyl had become a central part of the social fabric as Jews learned how to celebrate in the unfamiliar and unclaustrophobic setting of the suburbs. Postwar Jews had become fundamentally middle class en masse, an achievement not to be taken for granted when viewed against the flow of Jewish history in general, and the ashes of Eastern Europe in particular. The densely packed urban milieu in which Judaism could be experienced by osmosis had been traded up for the freshly painted promise and room to roam of the suburbs. There was no time to dwell on the past but only to look forward to the promise of a better tomorrow, to live lives based on the best that America had to offer—prosperity, consumerism, leisure, family, and happiness. . . .

Vinyl records fit wonderfully into this new reality, in which one of the central challenges was how to make a tract house feel like a Jewish home. What better way was there to accomplish this than via the record collection, which could be displayed in the newly purchased Formica record cabinet in the lounge? The genre of *freilach* (happy, cheery) music exploded to celebrate these good times. The covers reflect a commemoration of happy

Shmulik Fischer, Fraidele Lifschitz
Kum Sitz! A Jewish House Party
Menorah Records, c. 1960

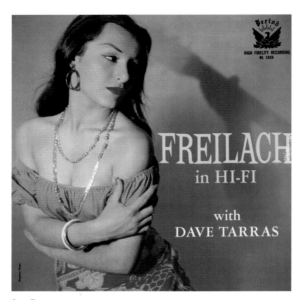

Dave Tarras
Freilach in Hi-Fi
Period Music Co., 1950

Various Arists
Freilach Tanze: For Wedding or Bar Mitzvah
Alshire International, c. 1970

Lou Klayman
Twistin the Freilach
Sonoder, c. 1960

Murray Lehrer and His Ensemble
Freilach in Hi-Fi Volume 2
Period Music Co., c. 1950

events, emphasizing the centrality of home, friends, and family. Jews could be playful, joyous, could eat, drink, dance, and sing, free from the emotion of fear that had dominated their lives over much of the last three millennia, while extolling the suburban lifestyle they had worked so hard to secure.

Within the hierarchy of festivities, none bought more joy than a wedding. Dashing grooms spin around their adoring, virginal brides before whisking them off to make Jewish babies on the cover of *Mazeltov: Wedding Songs of Our People—for My Beloved* by the wonderfully named Dukes of Freilachland. The Yiddish phrase in the corner of the album, *Zol zein mit glick,* wryly wishes the couple the good luck they will need in an era in which divorce was on the rise.

Jewish Wedding Dances, featuring Sam Musiker, uses a headless bride and groom to create an eerie "insert your face here" gimmick on the cover. The album promises not just authentic *freilachs* but also polkas, horas, shers, kozatskis, doinas, waltzes, and mazurkas, mixing in Ukrainian, Romanian, and Polish folk dances for an audience who appear to be a far more versatile and sophisticated set of dancers than those who perform the bump 'n' grind at weddings today. The dress style on these albums is modern and sophisticated. Men have often dispensed with their

kippot, or head coverings, in most cases, or if they are wearing them, they blend discreetly into the rest of their coiffure. The groups portrayed on these covers are as handsome a group as a room full of Jews can be. There is strangely no room at these events for the fat, aged, bald, ugly, infantile, or infirm.

Bar mitzvahs, too, required their own sound tracks. *Bar Mitzvah Favorites* featuring Harriet Kane highlights a glamorous mother wearing an off-the-shoulder creation in full profile while the bar mitzvah boy is reduced to an unfinished sketch, revealing who the star of the event really was. It is easy to mistake the depiction as a wedding with a very young groom. Evidently there was an audience of those who loved the sound of *simchas* so much that they purchased albums by the bands who played them. On the cover of *Marcus Goldman Orchestra,* Marcus Goldman himself looks confidently toward us, secure in the knowledge that his name is etched across both his signature accordion and the large velvet yarmulke he sports, suggesting that he is a man who is either extremely forgetful or heavily into personalizing his effects.

Why stop here? The happiness is just beginning to bubble over. *Kum Sitz! A Jewish House Party,* with its portrait of sedate, domestic, feminine, Americanized bliss, depicts a celebration of achieving the trappings of a subur-

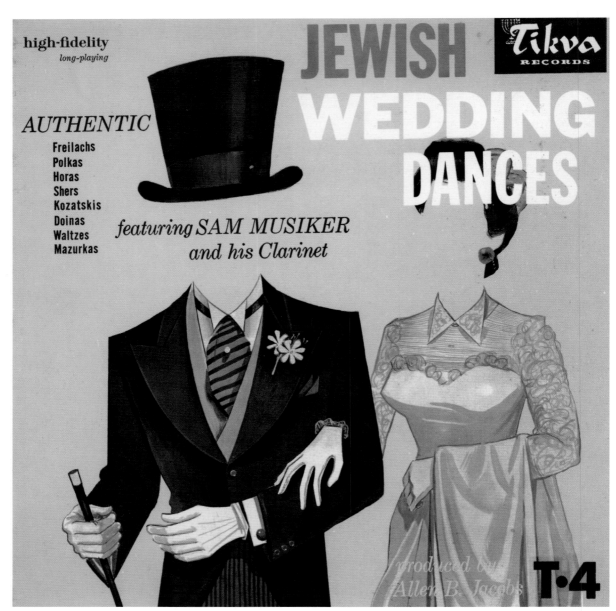

Sam Musiker
Jewish Wedding Dances
Tikva, c. 1960

Various Artists
Jewish Wedding Dances
Tikva, c. 1950

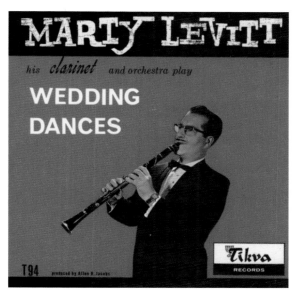

Marty Levitt
Wedding Dances
Tikva, c. 1960

Marty Levitt Orchestra featuring Harriet Kane
Bar Mitzvah Favorites
Tivell, c. 1970

Dukes of Freilachland
Mazel Tov
Aamco, c. 1950

ban lounge in which you can host friends and show off a record collection. One can almost smell the peculiar mix of mothballs and perfume. Saxophonist Paul Pincus offers *Music for Happy Occasions*, which evidently include three people looking at one gent doing a crazy dance, a kozatski perhaps.

And then there is Love. Dina Claire's breathtaking release, *The Jewish Heart*, showcases the singer, a stunning, wide-eyed blonde who looks, perhaps, so un-Jewish that the cover artist has thoughtfully surrounded her with stick drawings of Hasidic-looking shtetl dwellers. Our favorite album, *Jewish Rhapsodies for Those in Love*, by the Israeli Strings, has a nuzzling couple in dreamy soft focus. The impression that they are on their way to their boudoir to make mutually satisfying whoopee is only undercut, however, by the track list, which includes "O Mein Papa" and "My Yiddishe Momme." Few sounds are less likely to put you in the mood.

The final album in this chapter's collection is *Jewish Aerobics* by the Neshoma Orchestra, featuring a fresh-out-the-box pair of violet sneakers that doubtless coordinate with a matching velour Sergio Tacchini leisure suit hanging just out of shot. What could provide better motivation for you to get physical than working out to the very music that will be played at your son's bar mitzvah in a few weeks, a wonderful reminder that you need to lose at least twelve pounds if you are to look good in the photographs.

The Israeli Strings
Jewish Rhapsodies for Those in Love
RCA Victor, 1970

Paul Pincus and His Orchestra
Music for Happy Occasions
Mercury, c. 1960

Harry Ringler & His Orchestra
The Happy Soul of a People
Time, 1964

Dina Claire
The Jewish Heart
Algon, c. 1950

Jewish Music Alliance
Let's Sing
Tikva, c. 1960

Steve Fortgang and His Entertaining Orchestra
The Number 1 Bar Miztvah Band
Self-published, 1979

Marcus Goldman Orchestra
Self-titled
Al-Mar Records, c. 1980

The Stan Hiltz Orchestra
Kosher Style
World, c. 1970

Neshoma Orchestra
Jewish Aerobics
M. A. Productions, 1983

SPOTLIGHT ON:
America on the Roof

When Sholem Aleichem wrote his often gloomy *Tevye the Milkman* stories about Jewish village life in czarist Russia back in 1894, he could never have imagined what would go down over a century later. The year 2007 saw a really white girl from Orange County (Gwen Stefani) and an African-American rapper from Philadelphia with an Old Testament name (Eve) dressed in pirate lingerie and catwalking a fake plank on a fake ship with a crew of Tokyo hipster girls while singing a version of "If I Were a Rich Man," a song from a 1964 musical that turned his characters into singing icons of American popular culture.

This latest incarnation of the *Fiddler on the Roof* phenomenon was an ode to postfeminist bling, not Russian peasant striving; Eve and Gwen wanted a fancy house in London, not the few extra cows that would have changed Tevye's life. But such is the unprecedented arc of influence and inspiration that's been growing ever since Jerome Robbins first directed the play on Broadway in 1964. Perhaps because it was one of the first post-Holocaust representations of pre-Holocaust Jewish life, or perhaps because nostalgia is such a reliable cultural balm, or perhaps simply because nothing says a night at the theater like a singing Russian dairyman, *Fiddle[r]* enjoyed a record-breaking eight-year Broadway run (no[t] including four subsequen[t] Broadway revivals), inspired [a] 1971 smash-hit film, and wen[t] on to become what is easily th[e] most globally known, belove[d] and mocked piece of Jewish American cultural output eve[r]. No other Jewish anything ha[s] had a never-ending afterlife i[n] Norway, Rhodesia, Finlan[d], Mexico, Austria, Holland, an[d] Japan as *Fiddler* has.

Philip Roth may have right[-] fully decried it as "shtetl kitsch," but the quaint feel-goo[d] romance of Old World povert[y] (complete with a coming-t[o-] America happy ending) create[d]

[J]an Bart
[J]an Bart Sings Fiddler on the [R]oof
[T]ikva, 1964

The Barry Sisters
The Barry Sisters Sing Fiddler on the Roof
ABC-Paramount, 1968

Robert Merrill, Molly Picon, Stanley Black
Music from Fiddler on the Roof
London, 1968

Zero Mostel
Fiddler on the Roof
RCA Victor, 1964

the first true universal Fast Pass to American Jewishness.

It is no surprise, then, that *Fiddler* could fill its own chapter with LPs. Its songs have been covered by everyone from Ella Fitzgerald and Herb Alpert to the 101 Strings, Southern hip-hop act Cunnin Lynguists, and even the Temptations, who ripped through a nearly ten-minute medley of *Fiddler* tunes on their 1969 *On Broadway* TV special with Diana Ross & the Supremes. But we've chosen to feature only the full-length *Fiddler* recordings here—all those who decided that a solitary "Sunrise, Sunset" cover just wouldn't cut it.

Jan Bart Sings Fiddler on the

Roof is the only one that visually apes the original theater soundtrack, with its folksy water-color cover art that does its best to echo the Marc Chagall painting that gave the musical its name. The London production featuring Yiddish theater star Molly Picon kept Picon off the cover, which instead showcased yet another shot of Tevye—the Robert Merrill incarnation—in mid-rooftop dance (apparently he invented the sprinkler move). Mickey Katz, not one to romanticize tradition, literalizes the shtetl as a cartoon and replaces with Tevye with his own smiling face on his version of *Fiddler*.

By the end of the sixties, *Fiddler* was a such confirmed American pop product guaran-

teed to appeal to a national audience that its tunes had become must-covers, an instant set of new pop standards. Direct visual connections to the musical's Eastern European Jewish past were beside the point for Cannonball Adderley on his postbop jazz take on *Fiddler* and for Puerto Rican percussionist Joe Quijano, whose *Fiddler on the Roof Goes Latin* taught Tevye to mambo. Thanks to a little Broadway alchemy (and lots of collective cultural memory, guilt, and ethnic romance), the site-specific story of a world lost to pogroms and genocide had morphed into one of the twentieth-century America's greatest pop exports—the musical equivalent of the mighty bagel.

Roy Scott
Fiddler on the Roof Cha
Tribute, c. 1965

Joe Quijano
Fiddler on the Foof Goes Latin
MGM, 1965

Cannonball Adderley
Fiddler on the Roof
Capitol, 1965

Mickey Katz
Fiddler on the Roof
Capitol, 1965

CHAPTER EIGHT

THE SOUND OF SUFFERING: HOLOCAUST, SOVIET JEWRY, AND MARTYRDOM ON VINYL

For the better part of the past four thousand years, the world has not been too kind to the Jewish people. What finer way, then, for a Jew to feel validated when threatened than to draw the curtains and play some martyrdom vinyl? In addition to acting as a psychological placebo, the albums in this chapter play a variety of roles, from preserving and memorializing traumas of the past to delivering the news and mobilizing a community to ensure that it will not happen again. With their stark font choices, fire imagery, and liberal use of barbed wire, these covers could easily be mistaken for a collection of 1980s thrash metal bands. But back in the day, these albums were important expressions of identity and stark reminders of the dark side of the human condition; they coexisted side by side with all the *frailachs* and

Perry Como releases that would also be in the discerning person's record collection.

The bleak despair of the prewar Jewish mindset is beautifully captured on *The Jewish Mood* by Yiddish poet-artist Maxim Brodyn. The cover utilizes just about every shade of gray in the Pantone palette as the dismembered head of the artist gazes away somberly, surrounded by rough-hewn sketches of fellow Jews being chased down or left to cower in dark corners. In the wake of the Second World War and the destruction of six million Jews in the Holocaust, what is most surprising is that there is very little trace of it on vinyl. *Songs to Remember (Ghetto Songs),* released in the early 1950s by the wife-and-husband team Sarah and Hayim Fershko, is a rare exception and one worth exploring in greater depth. The

Maxim Brodyn
The Jewish Mood
n.d.

Sarah and Hayim Fershko
Songs to Remember (Ghetto Songs)
Tikva, c. 1950

cover features the dark charcoal design style that became de rigueur for Holocaust memory in the late sixties, but here it is somewhat incongruously juxtaposed with the smiling headshot of Sarah herself, suggesting that this album was less about memory and more about two performers building a career based on the songs that were familiar to them. This sense is reinforced by the liner notes, which fail to mention the horrific details of the performers' biographies. The Nazis had amputated their left arms at the shoulder as a punishment for entertaining the partisans during the war.

The liner notes of the Fershko album are notable for a second critical ellipsis. There is neither direct reference to the destruction of the Jews nor use of the word *Holocaust*—a term that did not become common parlance until the early sixties. Jews may have been ready to publicly mourn as Americans, a reality reflected by Leonard Bernstein's 1963 release of *Kaddish*, dedicated amid the general angst of the cold war to the "beloved memory of John F. Kennedy," but they were not able to do the same as they faced the Holocaust. The paucity of Holocaust vinyl reflects the psychological torment they experienced for a generation. It took nearly two decades before American Jews could publicly discuss the Holocaust and for it to enter their record collections.

The publication of Eli Wiesel's *Night*, a short but graphic depiction of life in the death camps, combined with the glare of the capture and trial of Holocaust supervisor Adolf Eichmann, changed all of this. The general unease around mention of the Holocaust was transformed into an immediate and desperate desire to keep memory alive, catapulting the destruction from the fringes to the center of American Jewish life. Memorials, commemorations, and ultimately museums were created, and this boom was reflected in the vinyl sphere with the birth of two new genres—the Holocaust album and the Soviet Jewry album in the late 1960s.

First came the straight commemorations. From the grand scale of Richard Tucker's cantorial *Yizkor: In Memory of the Six Million*, which was proudly presented on network television, to *Remember: Songs of the Holocaust*, released by the World Federation of Bergen-Belsen Survivors, albums flooded out, including *I Am a Zionist*, which presents one of the stronger arguments for being one—seven graphic black-and-white Holocaust images of the doomed and the dead set against a turgid brown cover. And then came the Soviet Jewry movement, addressing the plight of the one and a half million Jews vulnerable to the Kremlin's policy of persecution and imprisonment. American Jews were racked by regret

Leonard Bernstein
Symphony No. 3: Kaddish
Columbia, 1963

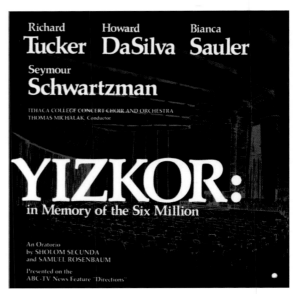

Richard Tucker, Howard DaSilva, Bianca Sauler, Seymour Schwartzman
Yizkor: In Memory of the Six Million
Ethnic Music Pub. Co., 1967

Trio Loránd
Songs and Tunes from the Ghetto
Supraphon, 1965

Emil Gorovets
I Am a Jew: Songs of the Martyred Yiddish Poets of Soviet Russia
Great Recording Co., 1977

Sidor Belarsky
Remember: Songs of the Holocaust
World Federation of the Bergen, 1961

Artist Unknown
I Am a Zionist
Unknown, 1975

Mikis Theodorakis, Maria Farandouri
The Ballad of Mauthausen: Six Songs
EMI, c. 1970

Dov Seltzer, Rivka Raz, Aric Lavive, Yona Atari
To Live Another Summer, to Pass Another Winter
Buddah Records, 1971

and remorse for failing to speak out loudly against the Holocaust. The bag of political tricks they had acquired from their involvement in the civil-rights movement was reinforced by the self-confidence they drew vicariously from Israel's triumph in the Six-Day War, set against the universal backdrop of the Cold War. They jumped at the chance for a do-over.

The alarm bells are rung by covers such as *The New Slavery* with its close-up shot of a knot of barbed wire echoing the Holocaust, and its clumsier appropriation of civil-rights imagery. *Silent No More* by Theodore Bikel defiantly claims to be based on tapes "smuggled out" of the Soviet underground, although the liner notes reveal either a hunger for universal affirmation or an effort at savvy marketing, as the record is promoted as less a Jewish album and more "a gem of a collectors album for Freedom Loving Human Beings." *Uvne Yerushalayim* by the neo-Hasidic performer Shlomo Carlebach makes the boldest statement of all, starkly connecting the Holocaust and the fate of Soviet Jews with the crude tag line "6 Million in Heaven, 3 Million in Hell."

The success of the Soviet Jewry movement was a deeply satisfying moment for American Jews. In liberating their imperiled brethren, they had proved to themselves what they could achieve politically and globally. The new sense of power born of the American Jewish experience would ensure that the Holocaust would never be allowed to happen again, reflected by the succinctly titled *Never Again,* with its design riffed off the Israeli flag hinting perhaps that the Jewish State was the long-term answer to Jewish safety. This stance is more succinctly and perhaps overconfidently captured by the approach of *Rabbi Meir Kahane of the Jewish Defense League Speaks,* an album in which the font size is dwarfed by the symbol of the Jewish star combined with an appropriated black-power fist.

The final album here is *And None Shall Make Them Afraid,* a veritable greatest hits album of Jewish defiance in the face of persecution, created by the fund-raising organization United Jewish Appeal in 1974. The album has tracks that run the gamut, covering threats to Israel, Holocaust memory, the "Theme Song of Jews Still in the Soviet Union," and even the granddaughter of writer Sholem Aleichem reading his poems. The cover is a confident statement—a fetching batik suggesting that wherever Jews were in peril around the world, the American Jewish community would rise up to protect their right to march en masse behind the Torah, despite the fact that this act of pious ritual devotion was of decreasing interest to the majority of American Jews themselves at this time.

THE NEW SLAVERY

Sherwood Goffin, Shlomo Riskin, Stanley Schwartz, Center for Russian Jewry
The New Slavery
Ariella Music, 1970s

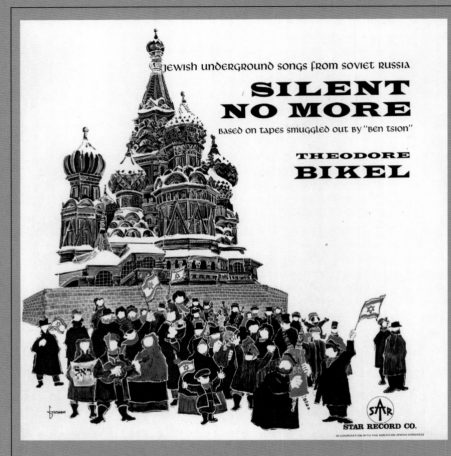

jewish underground songs from soviet russia

SILENT NO MORE

BASED ON TAPES SMUGGLED OUT BY "BEN TSION"

THEODORE BIKEL

STAR RECORD CO.

IN COOPERATION WITH THE AMERICAN JEWISH CONGRESS

Theodore Bikel
Silent No More
Star Records, 1971

Etgar Keret on "Pharaoh, Let My People Go" by Theodore Bikel from *Silent No More*

On first blush, this comes across like a bunch of guys playing banjo at the bottom of a well. But after a couple of listens, the secret power of the track becomes apparent.

It is a threat wrapped in a song. The performers manage to communicate such a mix of determination fused with craziness that no pharaoh would want to stand

in their way. The well sound is the kicker. This is where all our enemies will end up if they don't start showing some flexibility, pronto.

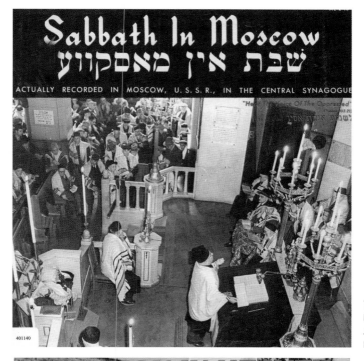

Yehudah Leib Levin, Menachem
Mendel Barkahn, Saul Karp
Sabbath in Moscow
Hebrew Sound & Vision, 1970s

Shlomo Carlebach
6 Million in Heaven, 3 Million in Hell
Menorah Records, 1970s

Meir Kahane
*Rabbi Meir Kahane of the Jewish
Defense League Speaks*
Fran, 1971

Bud Greenspan
Never Again
Flying Dutchman Records, 1971

"AND NONE
SHALL MAKE
THEM AFRAID"

Various Artists
And None Shall Make Them Afraid
United Jewish Appeal, 1974

CHAPTER NINE

HAIFA IN HI-FI: THE EVER-EVOLVING NOTION OF ISRAEL

The creation of the state of Israel in 1948 turned a revolutionary idea into a physical reality after two thousand years as an exilic dream. Jews around the world dutifully flocked to the nascent state from all quarters—from everywhere, that is, except the United States, where the Promised Land had already been discovered on the streets of Jamaica, Queens, Fairfax Avenue, Los Angeles, and Skokie, Illinois. The majority of American Jews sympathized with Zionism's goals, either out of emotional allegiance born of an age-old longing or in reaction to the still-fresh atrocities of the Holocaust. Yet they had no intention of moving to the place and were left to wrestle instead with the challenge of defining a meaningful relationship with the Jewish homeland from afar.

That Israel has had more record-cover image makeovers than Bowie and Madonna combined should not come as a surprise. The nation emerged in unresolved contradiction, unsure of its place between tradition and modernity, while attempting to be both a Jewish state and a democracy. The LPs that became cornerstones of Jewish record collections were equal parts ideological representation, vision statement, and identity expression, augmenting myriad other powerful symbols—such as shalom napkin holders, Western Wall tapestries, and Israeli craft trivets—that eventually flooded into Jewish homes.

Two albums from our collection demonstrate just how different these visions of Israel were. The 1940s release *Song and Soil* by the United Synagogue Chorus uses every golden

Karmon Israeli Dancers and Singers
Israel Sings!
Vanguard, 1966

United Synagogue Chorus
Song and Soil
United Synagogue of America, 1940s

William Gunther
Cocktail Hour in Israel
Request Records, c. 1950

shade of the sun to portray the pioneer state-builders taking a break from toiling the land to indulge in some spontaneous Israeli dancing. Collective life on the kibbutz was hard, but it was good. The Jews portrayed here are mission-driven, shirtless, unashamed of their bodies, and drunk with the pleasures of hand-plowing the land. Twenty years later, *Cocktail Hour in Israel* was released by William Gunther, a self-proclaimed "brilliant European pianist" whose specialty was to render "operatic music in highly unusual cocktail-bar style." The Israel here is Tel Aviv as Las Vegas, the biblical land promised by God to Abraham metamorphosed into a paradise for night club sophisticates who appreciate a mean martini. Zion had become, in the words of historian Jonathan Sarna, "a utopian extension of the American Dream." On one cover you can smell the eucalyptus and the camel dung, on the other, the liquor and cigarette smoke. Exactly what kind of state was Israel to be?

The two visions reflect the two sides of a debate that gripped the Jewish world through the first decades of Israel's existence. Should the national homeland be an ethical exemplar as a "light unto the nations" or an ordinary place that would normalize the Jewish condition and make its citizens as innocuous as the Dutch or Australians? In the famous words of the first prime minister, David Ben-Gurion, "When Israel has prostitutes and thieves, we'll be a state just like any other." The LPs that were produced and sold in record stores and synagogue gift shops, or brought back as souvenirs from the new country, tell the story of the evolution of this debate in vinyl. The pre-state portraits of British Mandate Palestine show that complexity and contradiction were present from the outset. From that era, the land is portrayed as a magical vision in which Jews are fine physical specimens, at one both with nature and a dazzling arsenal of agrarian tools, including a shepherd's crook on Shoshana Damari's *Voice of Israel* and a fearsome machete on *New Songs of Palestine*. All of the covers are different hues of blue, and a number depict eager Jewish families traveling with bags packed, on their way to the only place in the world where they could be masters of their own destiny. These covers were in marked contrast to the familiar images of the Jews of Eastern Europe, the ultimate in powerlessness, as well as the self-image of those buying the records in America, whose only journey was toward the middle-class comforts promised by careers in accountancy, medicine, and law.

Israel's founding coincided almost exactly with the birth of the mass-market LP. Vinyl was immediately used as a medium for Israelis eager to experiment with this new technology in order to show the world their land. Political leaders were early adopters. David Ben-Gurion was among the first to use an LP as a way to reinforce his standing in the American Jewish community. His decision to be portrayed shearing a sheep on the cover of *What Is a Jew?* was a reflection of the agricultural roots of the state. *Israel Is Born* sets the dignified Chaim Weizmann over a cartoon of the state filled with sheep, cattle, and primitive dwellings, promising voices of an all-star cast of prominent politicians, but still finding enough space to feature "actual scenes of daily life in Israel."

Early albums communicate a sense of the commitment and sacrifice that a nation of plucky immigrants dedicated to their collective mission. Jack Brass was a prolific folksinger who trumpeted himself as "the Burl Ives of Israel" while playing up his *halutznik* (pioneer) bona fides in his liner notes: "His music raised morale during the Blitzkrieg over London, he was then one of the first citizens to enter the concentration camp at Bergen Belsen, and the first to move to Israel to join an army where his songs worked their magic." The Trio Aravah's *Israel Today* has an impressive display of Israeli youth marching en masse in lockstep in

their best gym gear. Change the color of the flags from blue to red and the scene would not have been out of place in Red Square. The back cover proudly declares that although the trio were born in Lithuania, Poland, and Germany, they "represent an Israel that is developing its own culture that can truly be 'Israelism.'"

Albums were also a useful device to introduce the American audience to the geography of Israel. The LP covers proudly showcase the topographical differences between the desert around Ein Gedi and the agri-urban splendor of cities such as Haifa. This was achieved both subtly, as in Oranim Zabar's *On the Road to Elath,* and less so in *Songs of the Negev/Songs of Israel* by Lea Deganith, which went so far as to depict a set of signposts at a crossroads between Sodom and Eilat. The American Jewish appetite for these albums appeared to be insatiable. There was even a market for *Jerusalem's Synagogue Tour* by Yehezkiel Freiman.

Yet when Americans did start to come to Israel in droves, they did so not to live but to tour, a reflection of the increasingly sophisticated notions of leisure and vacation that were taking hold. The Jewish mambo pioneer Irving Fields released *Melody Cruise to Israel,* reinforcing the sense that the country was a

Shoshana Damari
Voice of Israel
Shoulsong, 1949

Abraham Wolf Binder
New Songs of Palestine
Keynote Recordings, 1948

Jennie Goldstein, Hymie Jacobson
Palestine Unser Heim
Deluxe, c. 1938

Moshe Nathanson
Sing—Palestine!
Metro Records, 1940s

Arthur Holzman
Israel Is Born
Caedmon, 1950s

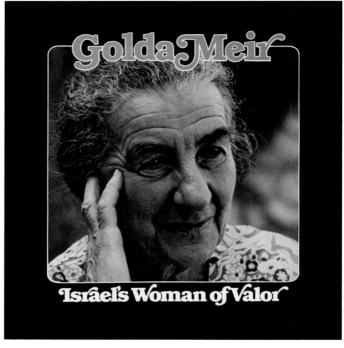

Golda Meir
Israel's Woman of Valor
Educational News Service, 1979

stylish Mediterranean port of call, attractive to Jew and non-Jew alike. Radio and television personality George Jessel appeared in a monocle and brandishing a cigar to give us *Seeing Israel with George Jessel,* on which he surveyed the land on our behalf. "Relax, close your eyes, and in an instant through the marvels of the electronic age you are wafted away to Israel. 'Sights' and sounds of Israel are brought to you in vivid detail, and you will enjoy a rocking-chair adventure which you can live over and over again merely with the flick of a button. You can almost smell the strange exotic scents of faraway places. Yes as you close your eyes and listen *you are there.*"

Other acts followed suit, exploring the Israeli terrain and reporting back to the endlessly fascinated American audience. A husband-and-wife act, Shimon and Ilana Gewitz, made it their mission to teach the songs of the state while also translating an array of popular hits from Brazil, Ireland, and Greece into Hebrew. The dynamic folk duo moved between Israel and Detroit and built a bridge between the two with a slew of releases proclaiming, for example, *Some of Our Best Songs Are Hebrew!* In an interview, Shimon took special delight in the duo's clothing, which, as hybrid in style as their music, was made by Ilana's own hand—"I describe our look as

Israeli meets folk international," he said. And the Barry Sisters sought to reassure their audience on the cover of their 1960s classic *Shalom* by appearing to jauntily step off a long-haul flight in tandem, arriving in an Israel that looked reassuringly modern—with not a hair out of place, carrying bouquets of fresh-cut flowers and ready to break into "Chiribim, Chiribom" at a second's notice.

One of the biggest barriers between American Jews and Israel was language, and vinyl did its best to break through. A slew of Teach Yourself Hebrew albums was released in response to one of the many miracles of the state's founding—the revival of Hebrew from the idiom of prayer and study to an everyday language and mother tongue. The well-intentioned producers of the the Listen 'N Learn language series appear not to have caught up with this revolution, creating a package that blurs all definitions of *Israeli, Jewish, Hebrew,* and *religion.* The album cover promises that the album is "Ideal for Easy Comprehension and Travel Communications" and that it offers "All you need to know to travel in Israel," yet it features a head shot of an avuncular figure, in ritual prayer shawl and *kippa,* bleary-eyed as if after hitting the *kiddush* table a little too hard at a bar mitzvah.

The language barrier was just one of a

number of complicated factors contributing to the low number of Americans "making aliyah," or moving to Israel, but the architects of the Zionist plan were a determined bunch, and they unleashed a barrage of creative strategies to reel in their American audience. A bevy of beautiful Israeli songbirds arrived to tempt young males to move to a promised land that appeared to be overpopulated by the 1950s equivalent of the Hooters girl—swarthy, chesty, feminine pioneers who toiled in the fields but were ready and willing to be known in a biblical way during the lunch break. These artistes flooded over like sirens sent to lure sailors onto the rocks, each one more enchanting and better endowed than the last. Shoshana Damari released the cleverly named *Haifa in Hi-Fi*, continuing the Israeli predilection for semi-accurate celebrity analogies, by marketing herself as the "Gina Lollobrigida of Israel." Hanna Ahroni, the product of a Yemenite father and Eritrean mother, was reputed to have been discovered singing her songs to her flock of sheep when she was a shepherd in Galilee. She cuts a ripe, exotic, and confident figure on the cover of *Songs of Israel*, laughing casually against the backdrop of a freshly harvested field of wheat.

If the female performers were authentically Israeli—free of American cultural influence—a slew of bands arrived that looked and occasionally sounded like American pop combos of the era. The Ayalons, named after a battle in the Israeli War of Independence, built an American following with twist, cha-cha-cha, and even calypso versions of hits such as "Falafel." The Sabras managed to effortlessly resemble an incarnation of a British guitar combo, the Shadows, and a quartet of trainee accountants. The fresh-faced crooner Avi Toledano ended up dedicating his career to winning the Eurovision Song Contest.

The popularization of Israeli folk dance added an experiential dimension to the music. A plethora of troupes such as the Dance Company Karmon and the Hadarim Israeli Dance and Song Theater were deployed to teach the world their exuberant yet infectious group choreography, and they performed to such popular tracks such as "Hineh Ma Tov" and "Dror Yikra." The flamboyance of their album covers is stunning. Coordinated, barefoot Jews are leaping and grinning in outfits that one member of the Karmon troupe, Yaffa Handel, described as "part biblical, part Arab, and part polyester, and ready to be ripped off in a second in-between dances." "Let us rejoice with Israelis. Folk Dancing belongs to all free people of all religions. Let us Dance!" proclaims *New Folk Dances of Israel*, an album

ORION

ORD 7143

DAVID
BEN GURION

WHAT
IS A JEW?

David Ben Gurion
What Is a Jew?
Orion, c. 1950

Trio Aravah
*Israel Today: Songs in
Hebrew by the Trio Aravah*
Capitol, 1970

Jack Brass
Israeli Folk Songs
Tikva, 1950s

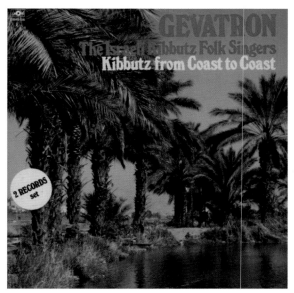

Oranim Zabar Israeli Troupe
On the Road to Elath: Songs of the Negev
Elektra, 1958

Lea Deganith
Songs of Israel
Capitol, c. 1950

The Israeli Kibbutz Folk Singers
Gevatron: Kibbutz from Coast to Coast
Hataklit, 1980

Yeheskiel Freiman
Jerusalem's Synagogue Tour
Hed-Arzi, 1960s

that came, as many of this genre did, with its own booklet of dance instructions so you could follow along at home and be transported by the power of dance to the fields of the Galilee.

In the dawn of the 1960s, two phenomena combined to make Israel, and Israeli vinyl, soar in popularity. The first was the release of the classic United Artists movie *Exodus*, directed by Otto Preminger and starring Paul Newman and Eva Marie Saint. The film, which turned the creation of the state into a heroic and romantic epic, was a box-office smash. Israel had at long last been given its Hollywood ending. A stirring soundtrack composed by Ernest Gold won an Oscar and quickly became an ever-present fixture in Jewish homes across the country. The phenomenal popularity of the movie and the album was a reflection of a deeper transformation in Jewish identity. For many Jews, Israel had supplanted traditional, synagogue-based ritual life. Indeed, following Israel had become a religion in its own right, with the country's political leaders replacing rabbis, newspaper headlines replacing Jewish texts, the Israeli flag replacing the Torah as a symbol, and the institutions and holidays of the Jewish state offering day-to-day authority and meaning—all of which could be reinforced by the spinning of a record.

Jews were not the only audience enthralled by *Exodus*'s telling of the miracle of Israel. The entire world was captivated by the resolve and resourcefulness of the near-victims of the Holocaust rising from the ashes to create a homeland. This sense of awe reached its apex during the Six-Day War in 1967, which began with fears of a second Holocaust and ended less than a week later with a decisive Israeli victory against the massed armies of the Arab world. *Life* magazine released a record-selling special edition packed with images of the conflict, which cast Israeli soldiers as veritable desert cowboys. The yarmulke became a fashion statement in the same way the Palestinian kaffiyeh would become two decades later. American Jews glued themselves to portable transistor radios, living for news broadcasts. Middle East geopolitics had become a hot topic, and it created a new genre of music—the war album.

The opening salvo of releases was recordings of the very radio broadcasts and commentaries that had thrilled Americans during the war itself. *The Battle for Jerusalem* boasts that it offers the Six-Day War "Recorded Live!" presenting listeners the opportunity to experience the sounds of war vicariously in the comfort of their own living rooms. Other albums offer faithful recordings of speeches of Israeli representatives, such as General (later President) Chaim Herzog, who became bona fide celebrities during the conflict.

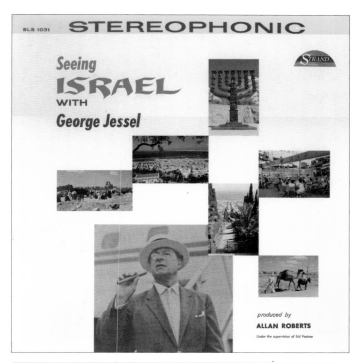

George Jessel
Seeing Israel with George Jessel
Strand, c. 1950

Irving Fields and His Trio
Melody Cruise to Israel
Oceanic, 1954

FAMOUS RECORDS INC.

FAM-1025

THE BALLADEERS

New Sounds of Israel

ILANA & SHIMON

The Balladeers: Ilana & Shimon
New Sounds of Israel
Famous Records, 1960

The digits *1967* appear to have been a magical marketing equation for vinyl. *Marches of the Israeli Defense Forces* rehashes previously issued material under the claim that it was "Just recorded and released in Israel in 1967." The savvy Ron Eliran keeps things fresh by releasing an album mysteriously entitled *1968,* on which he daringly sports civilian clothing—a fetching suede jacket—while entertaining exhausted soldiers in a frontline trench. Eliran was one of a number of Israeli performers whose careers received an adrenaline shot from the conflict. His track "Sharm el-Sheikh" and Naomi Shemer's "Yerushalayim Shel Zahav" (Jerusalem of Gold) became the theme songs of the war. Countless performers covered them, including Geula Gill and Yaffa Yarkoni, both of whom also jumped on the war-album craze. Even lesser known acts, like Meir Levy, donned camouflage to receive a recording contract.

The next wave of recordings to appear came courtesy of the Israeli Defense Force entertainment troupes, such as Lahakat Hanahal (the Nahal Band), which was a prolific star-making machine in Israel. Their album covers are a visual treat, creating the impression that this was a military force like no other. These Defense Force members were happier clowning in the desert, playing peekaboo among tomato plants in a greenhouse, and performing contortionist feats beside a pair of tanks, than they were waging war. Either the state was not yet comfortable with its newly realized power, or it knew that its power needed a softer spin.

For all the military displays on vinyl, there were few antiwar LPs, especially compared to the United States, where acts like Crosby, Stills & Nash and Joan Baez were busy building careers on them. One exception was the 1966 release *War Songs* by the beloved performer Chaim Topol, who was himself a graduate of the Nahal entertainment troupe. Topol had become influenced by the anti–Vietnam War movement and decided to release an antiwar album of his own, featuring the Natan Alterman song "Don't Give Them Rifles."

The song tells a story from the First World War. A soldier on his deathbed following a gas attack begs his nurse to promise that "when my children grow up, you won't let them use rifles." Alterman attempted to dissuade Topol from releasing the song, insisting that Israel's morale could not afford the luxury of an antiwar movement. Topol ignored the advice and released the album with its strong cover image of the performer singing into a grenade instead of a microphone. He later admitted that shortly before the Six-Day War, when the world was waiting for Israel to be crushed and rabbis blessed acres of farmland to prepare them as mass graveyards, he realized that Alterman had been right.

In the wake of the conflict, Israel was almost plagued by its own success. The country, now a regional superpower, was torn by internal debate about a long-term vision for the territories it had conquered and their inhabitants. On vinyl, the military bubble had burst, and in search of a next act, Israel played the only card it had left—to show it was more American than America, a state like any other state, pumping out lounge crooners such as Gadi Elon, known, according to the liner notes, "from the lounges of Las Vegas to the trenches of Tel Aviv," or seductive flight attendants whose come-hither looks suggested a level of tender care that would rival that of TWA and Pan Am.

The records occasionally put forward the face of a multicultural society not afraid to reveal its complexities through releases such as Rivka Raz's *Song of the Sephardi* or even *Sephardic Songs of the Balkans*, but most of the artists chose to keep things simple by presenting gaudy, happy images that papered over any cracks, offering *Big Hits from Israel* or, even more desperate to impress, *Lovely Israel*. The magical Israel Hit Parade series updated the "beautiful women in fields" strategy of the 1950s and '60s by providing their models with enormous pairs of orange headphones. *Israeli Disco Fever* attempts to fuse Travolta, the kibbutznik, and the world of disco (on the cover, the *fever* is translated into the Hebrew for "flu"). To cap the confusion, albums like *Shema Israel* by Sandra Sheskin began to appear. Sheskin co-opts the Western Wall, the most sacred and venerated Jewish holy site, using the Magen David as a frame for her own head shot. Only upon turning the album over do things fall into place. Sheskin may have been born and raised an Orthodox Jew in Baltimore, but her passion for the one god Yahweh floweth over to the extent that this record was a proud release of Messianic Records. According to the liner notes, Ms. Sheskin claims to "sing and channel the voice of God" as a Messianic Jew for Jesus, finding a place to fit her obligatory version of "Jerusalem of Gold" alongside "He Touched Me" (liner notes: "How the God of Abraham, Isaac and Jacob was made more real to me by the love of the Messiah") and "He Arose" ("The Messiah, the seed of David comes Alive"). The Jewish state has become a homeland at last. For Christian messianists, fundamentalists, and evangelicals, too.

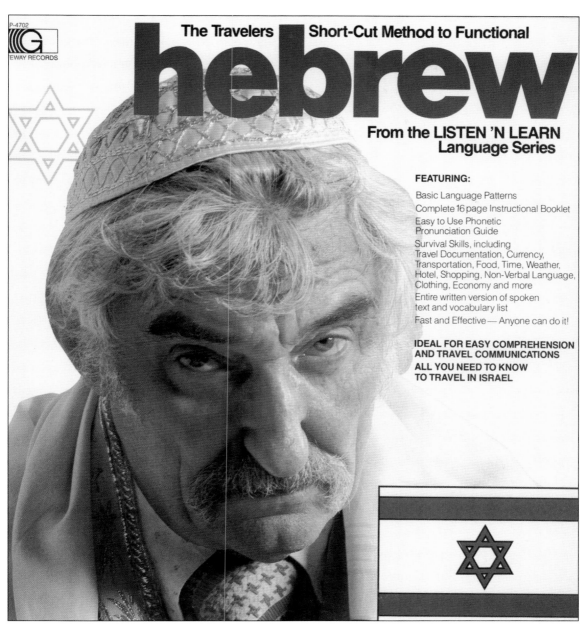

P-4702

EWAY RECORDS

The Travelers Short-Cut Method to Functional

hebrew

From the LISTEN 'N LEARN
Language Series

FEATURING:

Basic Language Patterns

Complete 16 page Instructional Booklet

Easy to Use Phonetic
Pronunciation Guide

Survival Skills, including
Travel Documentation, Currency,
Transportation, Food, Time, Weather,
Hotel, Shopping, Non-Verbal Language,
Clothing, Economy and more

Entire written version of spoken
text and vocabulary list

Fast and Effective — Anyone can do it!

**IDEAL FOR EASY COMPREHENSION
AND TRAVEL COMMUNICATIONS**

**ALL YOU NEED TO KNOW
TO TRAVEL IN ISRAEL**

Listen 'N Learn Language Series
The Travelers Short-Cut Method to Functional Hebrew
Gateway Records, c. 1970

HANNA
AHRONI

SONGS OF
ISRAEL

HI FI
DECCA
RECORDS

DL 8937   Printed in U.S.A.

Hanna Ahroni
Songs of Israel
Decca, 1962

Pierre Spiers
Hebrew Melodies in Popular Dance Time
Westminster Records, c. 1960

Shoshana Damari
Haifa in Hi-Fi
Seeco, c. 1960

Geula Gill
Geula Gill Sings Folk Dances of Israel
Menorah, c. 1960

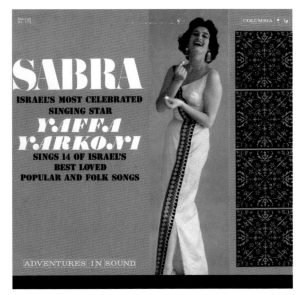

Yaffa Yarkoni
Sabra
Columbia, c. 1960

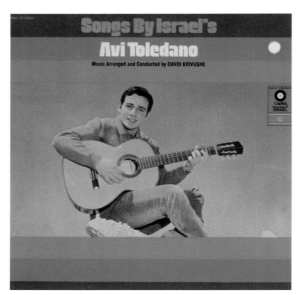

Avi Toledano
Songs by Israel's Avi Toledano
Capitol, 1968

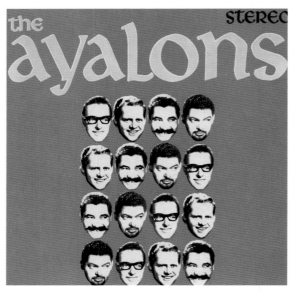

The Ayalons
The Ayalons Recorded Live
Vibra-sound recording studio, c. 1960

The Four Ayalons
Sing Along with Israel
Algon Theatrical Enterprise, 1962

The Barry sisters
Shalom
Roulette, 1962

The Sabras
Jerusalem of Gold
Tikva, c. 1968

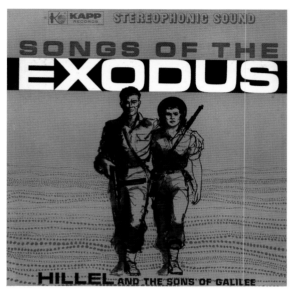

Hillel and the Sons of Galilee
Songs of the Exodus
Kapp, c. 1970

Mantovani
Exodus
London, 1961

Otto Preminger
Otto Preminger Presents Exodus
United Artists, 1960

Effi Netzer and Regina Zarai
Folk Dance in Israel Today
Collectors Guild, 1965

Karmon Israeli Folk Dancers and Singers
Songs of the Sabras
Vanguard Recording Society, c. 1950

Eliezer Adoram and Players of the Avia Theatre
Hava Nagila
Classic Editions, c. 1960

Israel Ensemble
We Are Here
Israel International Production Management, n.d.

The Hadarim Dance Ensemble
Songs and Dances of Israel Today
Capitol, c. 1960

Effi Netzer
This Is Israel: Israeli Folk Songs and Dances
P.Y.E. Records, 1969

Karmon Israeli Dancers and Singers
Folk Songs by the Karmon Israeli Dancers and Singers
Vanguard, 1968

CBS Israel Orchestra
Folk Dances of Israel
CBS, c. 1960

AUDIO RARITIES LPA 2470

The Battle for Jerusalem!

THE SIX DAY WAR

recorded live!

Alfred Eris and Russ Hall
The Battle for Jerusalem! The Six Day War
Audio Rarities, 1967

Topol
War Songs by Topol
London Records, 1966

Isaac Graziani; Israel Tseva Haganah le-Yisrael Band
Marches of the Israel Defense Forces
Columbia, 1967

Various Artists
The Six Day War: Original Radio Broadcast
CBS International, 1967

Various Artists
Six Days in June
Hataklit, 1967

Ron Eliran
1968
Hed-Arzi, 1968

Meir Levy
Meir Levy Sings Israel's Most Joyous Songs
Greater Recording Co., 1968

Jaffa Yarkoni
To Zahal with Love
CBS, 1967

Geula Gill
Songs After the 6-Day War
CBS, 1967

Southern Command Variety Ensemble
Untitled
Hed-Arzi, c. 1970

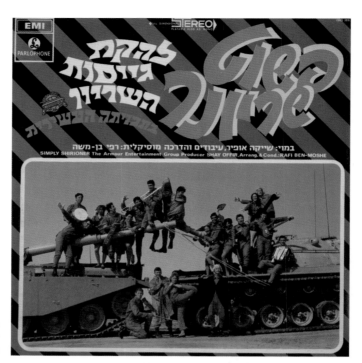

The Armour Entertainment Group
Simply Shrioner
EMI, c. 1970

The Nahal Variety Ensemble Group
Lahakat ha-Nahal be
Tokhnitah ha-21
Hed-Arzi, c. 1970

Various Artists
Israel Hit Parade 3
Hed-Arzi, c. 1975

Various Artists
Israel Hit Parade
Hed-Arzi, c. 1975

Various Artists
Israel Hit Parade 2
Hed-Arzi, c. 1975

Steven M. Reuben
Sing a Song of Zionism
Union of American Hebrew Congregations, c. 1970

Shayke Paikov
Lovely Israel Part Two
Isradisc, 1978

Various Artists
Hine Ma Tov
Hed-Arzi, 1970s

El Al
Hava Nagila Festival
CBS, 1974

Various Artists
Golden Songs of Israel
Columbia, 1973

Various Artists
Israel Disco Fever
Hed-Arzi, 1979

STEREO MM1061A

Sandra Sheskin
Shema Israel
Messianic Music, 1974

SPOTLIGHT ON:

Gadi Elon—A Lover, Not a Fighter

Certain performers have careers that epitomize the zeitgeist. Hendrix's career and death personify the freedom and danger of the sixties. The Sex Pistols reflect the social disorder of England in the mid-seventies. In the same way, the Israeli balladeer Gadi Elon illuminates the waxing and waning of the relationship between American Jews and Israel.

Born Gadi Pfefferbaum in Haifa, Elon was a graduate of the Israeli Navy's famed entertainment troupe, membership in which was a surefire shortcut to celebrity in the newly formed state. After his service, his fame was further burnished by his performances as Richard III in Hebrew at the National Theater. His life was good by Israeli standards, but the challenge of conquering America was impossible to resist.

Elon arrived in New York in the wake of the Six-Day War. The Jewish Military's miraculous exploits had placed a sense of the exotic around everything Israeli. Pioneering performers, including the soloists Yaffa Yarkoni, Shoshana Damari, and Ron Eliran had laid the groundwork and softened the market. The entrepreneur Avram Grobard, known also by his stage name, El Avram, had created a sprawling network of nightspots across the metropolitan New York area. Nightspots named Café Tel Aviv, Sabra East and West, and the Yaffa Café covered uptown and downtown, and clubs like Café Baba reached into Queens.

Life was a mix of the pragmatic by day, in which a crash course of English classes was a necessity, and the groovy delight that was the night. "Israelis were like heroes to America's cultural Jews back then. They would pack the clubs and hang on to our every word," Elon remembers. At midnight, the clubs would close, and the performers would descend upon the Olive Tree on Macdougal Street in the Village for an after-hours gig that would end at eight in the morning. "You would not believe the marathon jam sessions we had. Jewish and Arab performers bonding over music and reefer, fusing Sephardic, Yiddish, and Arab tunes. Everyone dancing on the table, knowing they would not be going home alone. This was like J-Date before there was a J-Date," Elon says.

But Gadi still harbored dreams of breaking out and becoming a universal star in the Neil Diamond mold, and he started to reconstruct his act, experimenting with more cosmopolitan sounds, such as "Sweet Caroline" and "My Cherie Amour." But the strategy backfired. "I was caught in a trap. Israeliness was what made me different from all the other international acts doing the circuit. But the Israeli mar-

Gadi Elon
Live
Isra-Art Productions, 1975

let was now hooded. It felt like every young Israeli who knew the words to "Hava Nagila" and could play three chords on the guitar was over here."

Gadi cracked this conundrum in 1970 with the release of *Sing, O Beloved Land*. The genius of the album was simple. Using his language lessons to good effect, he sang the familiar Israeli songs in English. No less a light than *Variety* praised the way "Elon sings Hebrew lyrics and then sings the line again in English for his audiences' benefit." Elon had his big break. The album, which had been recorded in the legendary Electric Lady Studios thanks to an Israeli recording engineer who let him in through the backdoor, sold over forty thousand copies and, better yet, got him invited to headline the National Hadassah convention. "Picture four thousand women dancing in the aisles. For the next four years, there was not a

Hadassah luncheon taking place anywhere in the country without Gadi Elon," he remembers proudly.

Elon began to live out of a suitcase, leaping around the country from gig to gig while mastering the art of American stagecraft: how to work the crowd and leave them spellbound with a delicate balance of humor, song, and tears. "The true spirit of Israel plays on the strings of their heart. My recipe was to be bigger than life, to talk a lot about miracles and layer on the schmaltz. American Jews love a lot of schmaltz." But the glory days came to a screeching halt after the Yom Kippur War in 1973. Israel, though victorious, had its aura of invincibility and self-confidence shaken by the conflict. According to Elon, "Israelis began to simply imitate the pop sounds of the United States and England. Our country and our music became spiritless."

But Elon was resilient enough to overhaul his act once more. "I realized that Israel had a problem imagewise. Israelis were seen as fighters, not lovers, which was a terrain monopolized by French and Italian performers." So he used an American-style wardrobe modeled after Paul Newman's to try reclaim a lover's image. "Everything owned seemed like it was made of green velvet." His act also changed. "I relied upon nostalgia, giving an older audience exactly what they wanted—Israeli spirit circa 1967." His 1976 eponymous album captures this period, in which he played Caesars Palace in Vegas as an opener for Alan King. The album showcases his act. Side one is a set of Israeli favorites. Side two is a set of universal classics, including "Put a Little Love in Your Heart" and "You Are So Beautiful." The cover was shot in the woods at his father in

Gadi Elon
Self-titled
Elon Creative Productions LTD, 1978

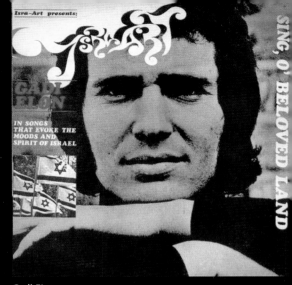

Gadi ELon
Sing, O Beloved Land
Isra-Art Productions, 1971

law's house in Westchester. "I am all lover here," he claims. "Whether the love I sang about was for the ladies or for Israel, it was one and the same. When I sing about how much I love Jerusalem, the city could be a metaphor for a woman in the same way Pat Boone sang about Jesus."

But Elon knew his market was collapsing. The Catskills were in their death throes. Lounges were closing. Disco was decimating everything in its path. "This was a scary and depressing time. My audience literally evaporated overnight." Elon made one last desperate effort to shed his aging fan-base by relocating to Vegas and repackaging himself as a universal balladeer, but his heart was not in it. "I had become labeled as a Jewish performer, and could not break the middle-American market."

Again he faced a turning point in his career. His future seemed destined to lie in the novelty gifts business. But then an associate from the music industry asked him to come down to Pensacola, Florida, to be a cantor for the High Holy Days. Gadi relished the role. " made the temple hop with emotion. The congregants said that when Gadi talks to God God answers him." He took the job full-time. "I see the job o the cantor as a guaranteed chance to perform every Saturday. I experience the same excitement as when was playing a nightclub except the audience is the same every week."

CHAPTER TEN

STOP SINGING OUR SONGS: NON-JEWISH MASTERS OF THE JEWISH MELODY

From the biblical Moses's coming of age as the Egyptian Pharaoh's grandson to Madeleine Albright's familial amnesia, passing as a non-Jew has been something of a Jewish tradition. A history of anti-Semitism, brutal suffering, and diasporic wandering pretty much guaranteed that that the traffic was mostly one way. With all of the hardship, what would make anyone want to pretend to be a Jew?

All of this changed in 1950s America when the social, economic, and cultural progress achieved by Jews in the postwar period had reached such a pinnacle that social philosopher Will Herberg could make the case in *Protestant, Catholic, Jew* that modern American society was based on three pillars—one Protestant, one Catholic, and one Jewish. After centuries of being outsiders, Jews had become part of the establishment, despite comprising just 4 percent of the population. Musically, the Jewish community was so close-knit and their appetite for consumption so insatiable that they formed an enticing target market for non-Jewish performers to create vinyl that either was overtly Jewish or simply explored Jewish themes.

The gold standard of this genre is *Connie Francis Sings Jewish Favorites*. The 1961 album by this Italian-American, born Concetta Rosa Maria Franconero, became one of the best-selling Jewish musical recordings of all time. The album cover showcases the vaguely Semitic good looks of one of teenybop rock and roll's first hit machines. Her sobbing signature style on tracks such as "Who's Sorry Now?" and "Where the Boys Are" had already

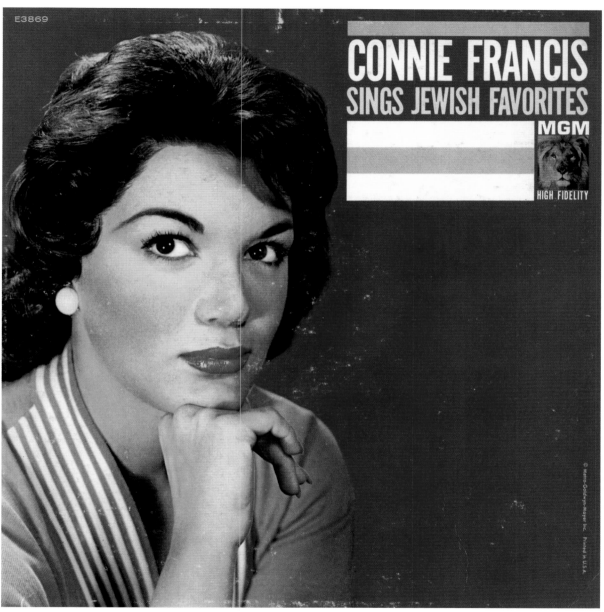

E3869

CONNIE FRANCIS
SINGS JEWISH FAVORITES

MGM
HIGH FIDELITY

Connie Francis
Connie Francis Sings Jewish Favorites
MGM, 1960

WHAT IT SOUNDS LIKE

FOR THE FIRST TIME IN THE HISTORY OF JEWISH MUSIC
JON YUNE

ose shalom

OSE SHALOM
RACHEL
SUKI YAKI
CANTOR OF SHABBOS
SISU VE'SIMCHU
SHMA ISRAEL
ARIRANG
RUMANIA
BASHANA HABAAH
JERUSALEM OF GOLD
A YIDDISHE MAMA
MAYIM MAYIM
RAD HALYLA
TSENA TSENA
ZAMAR NODED

Jon Yune
Ose Shalom
Shai Productions, 1960s

Norman Lear on Jon Yune's *Ose Shalom*

I was thoroughly engaged with Jon Yune and Ose *Shalom* from the first cut on the album, not so much remembering the individual songs as being stirred by the joy and the warmth and the love they evoked. As I listened, I was sure I'd have felt the same were I not a Jew. And then along came "My Yiddish Mama." Suddenly I was crying, and my grandmother, my *baba,* long gone, was in the room with me. I'd skipped a song and gone back to it; it was titled "Cantor of Shabbos," but as a boy I'd known it as "Oy, Ot Er Gedavent" and now I was weeping like a baby. It was my grandfather's, my *zada*'s, all-time Yiddish favorite. There they were, Baba and Zada, crying too, their arms around me.

made her America's sweetheart. This disk features pitch-perfect renditions of songs such as "O Mein Papa," "My Yiddishe Momme," and "Yossel, Yossel." For a woman who claims she is "10 percent Jewish on her manager's side," her mastery of Yiddish and Hebrew is almost flawless; only once does she slip into her Newark drawl on "Shein vi de Levone" (Beautiful as the Moon).

Italian Johnny Puleo is also pitch-perfect on his rendition of "Yussel, Yussel" on *Jewish and Israeli Favorites*. But his task is a little easier as he blasts through his twelve tracks on a harmonica with his backup band, the Harmonica Gang. The harmonica sound was in vogue at this time, and there was a slew of bands competing within the genre, from Jerry Murad's Harmonicats to the Strnad Brothers of Flint, Michigan, who became known as the Strand Brothers because their name was so often misspelled that way. Puleo used his dwarf-size stature—he was four feet six inches tall—to ensure that his band stood out from the pack. Surrounded by his gang, he grins from the front of the album, wearing a cowboy hat and chaps, his harmonica in a specially made holster, ready to be drawn at a second's notice.

Another Italian American overcome by the desire to explore his "Jewish side" was Pierono (Perry) Como, the master of the Christmas

album, and the artist behind the 1953 release *I Believe: Songs of All Faiths Sung by Perry Como*. On the track list, "Good Night, Sweet Jesus," and "Nearer, My God, to Thee," stand shoulder to shoulder with "Eli, Eli" and "Kol Nidre." The liner notes choose to ignore the fact that the last two tracks are Jewish, citing them simply as "examples of a darkly emotional strain, [that] are chanted by Perry with all the somber dignity inherent in their music."

A pre-National Rifle Association Charlton Heston—whose chiseled jaw Cecil B. DeMille once compared to that of Michelangelo's *Moses*—also makes little use of the word *Jewish* on his double-album release *Charlton Heston Reads "Out of Egypt" from the Five Books of Moses of the Holy Bible*. The liner notes make it clear that it is the immense thespian talent of Heston, not the religious significance of the Bible, that is given top billing. "To his readings of the Hebrew Bible, Charlton Heston brings the same qualities that have made him beloved by millions for his portrayal of Moses in the motion picture *The Ten Commandments* and of Ben-Hur in the movie of the same name."

Jewish themes were explored in a more subtle fashion by the conservative born-again Christian hitmaker Pat Boone, who dons a red cardigan and adopts a choirboy pose on *Pat*

Boone Sings Irving Berlin. Berlin, born Israel Isidore Beilin or Baline, the son of an immigrant cantor, allegedly claimed that "Pat Boone sings these songs exactly as I would like to hear them sung." Boone was no stranger to the Jewish repertoire—he also wrote the lyrics to "Exodus" about a decade before putting out his *Songs for the Jesus Folks* album.

Almost as unexpected is Johnny Cash in a 3-D image on the cover of his 1969 recording, *The Holy Land.* The concept album, which was partly recorded on site in Israel, is a meditation on the role of religion in life, concluding with the spectacular track, "God Is Not Dead." Cash had just released the legendary *Johnny Cash at Folsom Prison,* the title cut of which cemented his reputation as a world-class sinner, but here the Man In Black is reborn as a saint wearing a black frock coat and white turtleneck, framed by oak trees against an Israeli backdrop.

The Korean singer and comic Jon Yune appears in a proud, stoic portrait on the cover of his 1975 release, *Ose Shalom,* which features Yune doing some of the biggest hits of the Hebrew and Yiddish songbook, all in the original languages. The album plays up the cross-cultural improbability with its "For the first time in the history of Jewish Music"

tagline. Yune chose to be photographed in front of the United Nations building. In his words, "I could sing in sixteen different languages and I wanted to have a symbol of the whole world there, but especially the American flag, because only in this country could a Korean guy sing Hebrew and Yiddish Songs." Of all of the songs in his repertoire, Yune's version of "Exodus" still means the most to him. Yune sees a parallel between the history of Jews in Israel and the Japanese rule over Korea. To this day he still closes his Vegas shows with the song, out of solidarity. Of course, Yune's Jewish identification is also easy fodder for some old-fashioned stand-up shtick:

I was married to my Jewish ex-wife for one year. It didn't work because Confucius said, "When you marry, you have to know how to treat your wife. You must treat her kindly and gently, as if she's your guest." I treated her like a guest, and she checked out! She didn't know one word of Yiddish! I was sick and tired of teaching her! She was like a shiksa. You know, a "shiksa." It's an electric razor. Now I'm married to a shiksa, a Korean girl, she's an electric razor. She cuts me so many different ways, I almost think I'm Jewish.

Johnny Puleo and His Harmonica Gang
Jewish and Israeli Favorites
Audio Fidelity, 1961

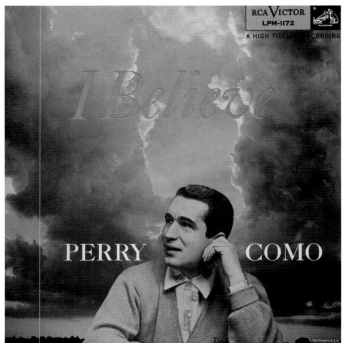

Perry Como
I Believe
RCA Victor, 1956

Pat Boone
Pat Boone Sings Irving Berlin
Dot, 1957

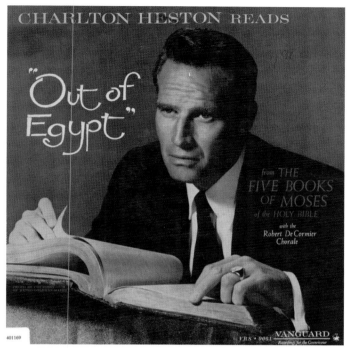

Charlton Heston
Charlton Heston Reads "Out of Egypt"
Vanguard, 1960

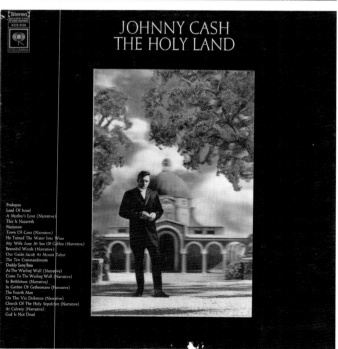

Johnny Cash
The Holy Land
Columbia, 1969

CHAPTER ELEVEN

THE FOLK EXPLOSION:
THE LAST DAYS OF JEWISH VINYL

When the folk music revival began wafting out of the coffeehouses of Greenwich Village in the 1950s, its bohemian messages of political awareness, community, and tolerance of all things paisley were particularly attractive to the young Jewish audience. These Jews had come of age knee-deep in the suburban lifestyle that was the embodiment of the middle-class establishment. Among those quickly acquiring black turtlenecks and berets, there were a number who believed they could harness the values of peace and love that were in the ether and use them to revitalize their own identities. The nascent freedom to talk openly about the Holocaust, as well as a resurgent pride in Israel, made this a fertile time for renewal and renaissance. A group of young rabbis and political activists had just created the Havurah movement, rebelling against the empty spirituality they had experienced in the suburban synagogues of their youth. Letting their freak flags fly, they fused Torah study, prayer, and an excess of scatter cushions to organize small, egalitarian communities. A similar spirit was breathing a new energy into the Jewish music scene. Cantorial and Yiddish LPs were widely viewed as déclassé, making this the perfect opportunity to refashion Jewish sound by using the style of the day to retain relevance and engage a new audience at the same time. After all, if black was beautiful, why couldn't Judaism be too?

Judaism had always had an authentic folk music tradition with its roots in Eastern Europe. Jewish folk was a mix of religious, Yiddish secular, and early Zionist classics. It

The Rabbis' Sons
To Life
EMES, 1968

Martha Schlamme
Martha Schlamme Sings Jewish Folk Songs Vol. 2
Vanguard, c. 1950

Hillel & Aviva
Land of Milk and Honey: Israeli Songs
Riverside, 1956

The Yemenite Trio
Israel Folk Songs
Tikva, 1960s

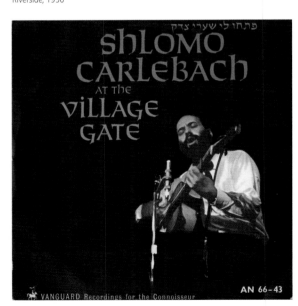

Shlomo Carlebach
Shlomo Carlebach at the Village Gate
Vanguard, 1963

had been synthesized and kept alive in the United States, often in sing-along style by the likes of Martha Schlamme, who looked as though she had raided Joan Baez's wardrobe for the cover of her fifties classic *Martha Schlamme Sings Jewish Folk Songs Vol. 2*, as she mesmerizes and soothes her children, one reclining awkwardly on the fireplace. In Israel, folk music was undergoing somewhat of a parallel renaissance at this time, driven by the need to popularize the reborn Hebrew language and embrace the ideology of Zionism, while eradicating the vestiges of Yiddish, considered a weak tongue besmirched by the Eastern European experience. Electric guitars were in scarce supply in Israel, so the folk sound was the perfect mechanism to achieve this aim. The husband-and-wife team Hillel and Aviva are a good example of the era and were one of the first folk duos to record in the early 1950s, Hillel with his deep voice and beguiling mastery of the shepherd's flute, the chalil, accompanied by Aviva on the goatskin drum.

It was Shlomo Carlebach, a prolific songwriter and master of Hasidic melody, who began to combine the American folk movement with Jewish tradition. He moved to Berkeley from Greenwich Village, where he had rubbed shoulders with Bob Dylan, Joan Baez, and Peter, Paul and Mary. He fused their messages of peace and love with Hasidic melodies, coining the term "holy hipplach" (a Yiddish version of "holy hippie") along the way. His 1963 album *Shlomo Carlebach at the Village Gate*, recorded live at the iconic folk nightclub, incorporates blues with folk to create a sound that is sacred but distinctly American. The liner notes reinforce the sense of something sacred occurring in this hotbed of folk music: "Never before had that sprawling offbeat musical cavern—packed to its subterranean seams—seen such scenes . . . exuberant fans . . . swayed to and fro in a frenzy of compulsive participation."

But Carlebach was not alone. The Noam Singers, a clean-cut, well-tailored group who swung between being a trio and a quintet, proudly boasted of representing "The New Dimension in Hebrew Music" on their cover. The Rabbis' Sons were a boon for lovers of truth in advertising: The members of the band look exactly like a group of rabbis' sons. They are pictured at an off-kilter angle, standing somberly on the edge of a forest, a serious band with a serious motivation. "These songs will hopefully lead the modern listener to a new deeper appreciation of yearning and faith, ecstasy and inspiration that pervade Jewish prayers and Jewish music," the liner notes declare. "They strive to fill some of the emptiness of the secular." The Dudaim—Hebrew for the Mandrakes, the mandrake being a biblical symbol of fertility—emerged from Israel in the wake of the 1956 Sinai campaign, their sweet harmonies of love and hope a subtle juxtaposition to the pomp of the traditional war songs of the time.

And then Bob Dylan changed it all. Any debate about the most seminal moments in modern music history will inevitably lead to Bob Dylan's decision to ditch his folk roots and "go electric" at the Newport Folk Festival in 1965. Its influence on both authentic folk music and rock and roll has been dissected by music fans and scholars ad nauseam. Little has been written about the shift it effected within the Jewish music scene. Its impact appears to have been visible as well as audible. The clean-cut look of the recording artists went out the window. Acts strove to be less buttoned up, each developing its own signature style, affecting images that were ever shadier, more mysterious, and more dangerous. The Messengers don raincoats and pose on the waterfront for their *"In" Jewish Sound* album, The Chosen Ones model early Merseybeat jackets and turtlenecks, and Kesher ape the Byrds, peeking out from the shadows in their photo shoots for their eponymous release, warning in prankster style in their liner notes

that the "General Surgeon has determined playing of this record on Shabbes or Yom Tov is dangerous to your spiritual health." The Zim Brothers, perpetual showmen, unleash their psychedelic side on *Peacing It Together,* proving that they are "able to talk TODAY's LANGUAGE here and now exciting groovy sounds for a whole new generation of today people."

Typical of the times was the five-piece band Ruach ("spirit" in Hebrew), who adopt what vocalist Ira Eisenman refers to as their "fighting pose" on the cover of *Volume I.* For Eisenman, the band was influenced by the sounds of the day—James Taylor, Crosby, Stills, Nash, and Young, and the Turtles—and wrote songs that fused their melodies and the band's Modern Orthodox value system, creating music that they hoped would do some religious outreach. The combination was well received. The popularity of their anthem, "Puff the Kosher Dragon," a tribute to Peter, Paul and Mary, drew over six thousand to a gig at Brooklyn College over Sukkoh, an evening which Eisenman calls their Budokan, referring to the Dylan album *Live at the Budokan.*

Israel became a veritable production line for acts during the mid 1960s. Although they look like a trio while posing with a donkey (in a cover shoot that, believe it or not, took place on Long Island) on *Donkey Debka!* Ran Eliran

Columbia
8579

Bob
Dylan

You're No Good

Talkin' New York

In My Time of Dyin'

Man of Constant Sorrow

Fixin' to Die

Pretty Peggy-O

Highway 51

Gospel Plow

Baby, Let Me Follow You Down

House of the Risin' Sun

Freight Train Blues

Song to Woody

See That My Grave Is Kept Clean

© COLUMBIA RECORDS 1962

Bob Dylan
Self-titled
Columbia, 1962

The Noam Singers
The New Dimension in Hebrew Music
Tikva, 1967

The Rabbis' Sons
Self-titled
EMES, 1967

The Dudaim
Ben and Adam
Elektra, 1960

Malka & Joso
Jewish Songs Hebrew and Yiddish
Tower, c. 1970

and Nehama Hendel had originally been hand-plucked from obscurity by Ed Sullivan, who was looking for acts to appear on his show in celebration of Israel's tenth anniversary. Rebranded as Ron and Nama they found a degree of fame in North America that eluded them in Israel until they took Joan Baez's hit "Donna Donna" and made it a success back home. Fewer songs tell a better story about the cross-border popularity of folk music. Baez had originally sung the tune in an English translation of a Yiddish original, and then Ron and Nama sang it in Hebrew. Not bad for a song that uses the image of a calf going to the slaughter as a metaphor for the Holocaust.

The Parvarim ("Suburbs") were known as Israel's Simon and Garfunkel because they physically resembled the American duo, translated their material into Hebrew, and even split up, though not because of musical differences but because one of them became Ultra-Orthodox. The Ofarim also came to an unhappy rock-and-roll ending. Esther, the wife in this Israeli-born couple, parlayed her minor role in the movie *Exodus* into representing Switzerland in the 1963 Eurovision Song contest. They tried to use their second-place finish as a springboard to stardom. After their 1967 folk-rock smash, "Cinderella Rockefella," became number one in Britain (they were the

first Israelis to reach those giddy heights), the Ofarim went on to sell over a million copies across Europe. However, they never again looked as suave as they did on the cover of that album in their silver wonderland. As in many sixties rock tales, husband Abi fought drug addiction, and their careers never recovered.

The truth was, by 1970 the folk revival was running out of steam, being replaced by the edgier rock sounds of Mordechai Ben David or the magnificent prog-rock vibes of Judea. Just as the cantorial baton was passed on to a younger new school, the folk mantle was inherited by large troops of musical upstarts who wielded guitars en masse and looked like precursors of bands like the Polyphonic Spree. The NFTY Levites cover might as well have been an homage to soul greats the Five Stairsteps (of "Ooh Child" fame). *The Edge of Freedom* features some of the finest electric guitar work you will find on any Jewish album, but the cover is the Jewish equivalent of the *Abbey Road* cover, provoking more questions than it answers. Why are the women barefoot but not the men? Why is one of the female vocalists sporting a wide yellow tie? What in the world is making the male vocalist nearest the wall jerk his head to the side and grin like that?

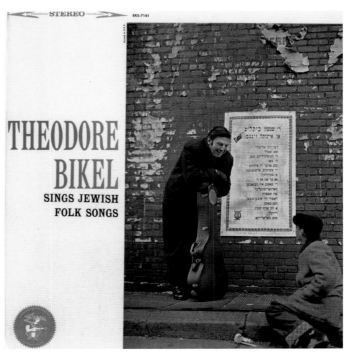

Theodore Bikel
Theodore Bikel Sings Jewish Folk Songs
Elektra, 1959

Theodore Bikel
Theodore Bikel Sings Songs of Israel
Elektra, 1958

The Chosen Ones
Self-titled
Fran, 1968

The Mark 3 Orchestra and Singers
The New Jewish Sound
Fran, 1966

The Messengers
The "In" Jewish Sound
HY Records, 1969

Kesher
Self-titled
Self-published, 1984

The Brothers Zim
Peacing It Together
Menorah, 1972

Rashi and the Rishonim
Self-titled
Fran, 1971

Ruach
Self-titled
Self-released, 1981

The golden age of Jewish folk music may well have been drawing to a close, but there were still those smart enough to pick up the crumbs. On the Esther Jungreis album *You Are a Jew,* an LP recorded live after her 1973 Madison Square Garden appearance, the rebbetzen gazes sternly out from the cover, beautiful and commanding at the same time. The album is a masterstroke of marketing, alternating between berating the target audience— "IF YOU ARE JEW THEN YOU OWE IT TO YOURSELF TO LISTEN TO THIS RECORD!"— and then soothing them: "For maximum impact to be listened to in the stillness of the night." But most important, Esther was in touch with her audience and knew the promises the folk music era had failed to deliver: "The Rebbetzen believes that now more than ever young people are ready to accept their responsibility as Jews. Having tasted affluence and experienced the drug culture, they hunger for something spiritual." This is an album that is both confident and optimistic, cocksure that a brighter tomorrow lay around the corner. The Beatles had the Maharishi. The Jews, it seemed, had Esther Jungreis.

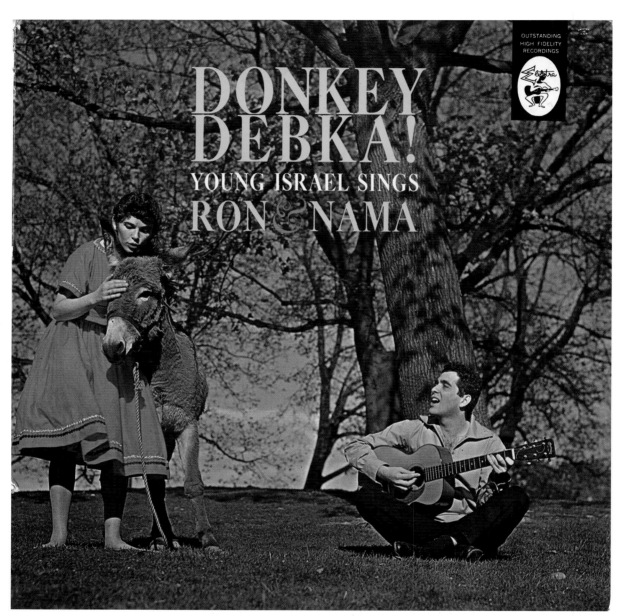

Ron & Nama
Donkey Debka! Young Israel Sings
Elektra, 1959

Ron and Nama
Sabra the Young Heart of Israel
Elektra, 1960

The Parvarim
The Parvarim Sing Simon and Garfunkel (in Hebrew)
CBS, 1972

The Lirons
Self-titled
Noam, 1975

Ilan & Ilanit
Shuv Itchem
Hataklit, 1972

WHAT IT SOUNDS LIKE

Esther & Abi Ofarim
Cinderella Rockefella
Philips, 1963

Shalom Auslander on Abi and Esther Ofarim's "Cinderella Rockefella" from *Cinderella Rockefella*

It's like I've taken some sort of magical pill that has removed all cynicism, negativity, and despair from my psyche. It worries me for a moment, but only for a moment, and soon I can't help but embrace it. "I love your chin!/Say it again!/I love your chinny-chin-chin!" Me too, baby. Me too.

Shalom Rav
Kol B'Seder in Concert
Sound Decisions, 1982

Duo Reim
Chassidic Goes Pop
London, 1972

Wilshire Boulevard Temple Camps
Cherish the Torah
NCR Records, 1976

Sarah Sommer Chai Folk Ensemble
Chai Is Hebrew for Life
Self-published, 1974

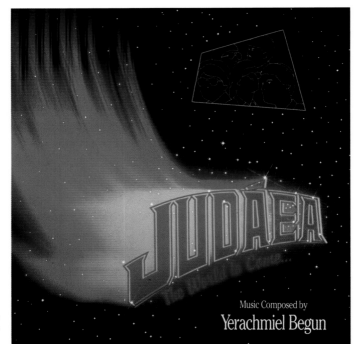

Yerachmiel Begun
Judaea: The World to Come
Self-published, 1981

Mordechai Ben David
Moshiach Is Coming Soon
Gal-Rpn, 1975

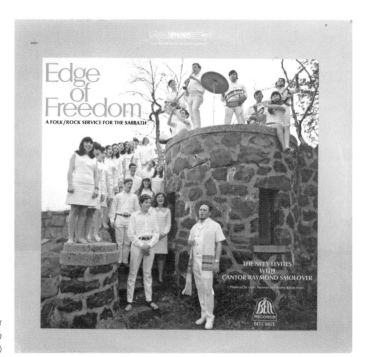

The NFTY Levites with Cantor Raymond Smolover
Edge of Freedom
BellRecords, c. 1970

Esther Jungreis
You Are a Jew
Hineni, Inc. , 1973

SPOTLIGHT ON:

The House That Theo Built

In 1958, a thirty-two-year-old theatre actor and rising folk-music star named Theodore Bikel headed down to New York's Lower East Side to shoot the cover of his fourth album for Elektra Records, *Theodore Bikel Sings Jewish Folk Songs*. Bikel's first move was to create a fake theatrical poster with all the song titles written out in Yiddish, billing himself only as "The Grandson of Reb Shuman Bikel." That's where the earnest bid for Jewish authenticity ended.

"They had me leaning on a guitar talking to a little kid," says Bikel. "But there were no Jewish kids wandering around at the time, so I said to this little kid, *'yingele,* come here,' and he said, *¿Que quiere?* He was Puerto Rican, but he looked Jewish, so he sat there for us. Then I figured that no brick wall without graffiti is authentic, so I took a crayon and wrote three Hebrew letters on the wall that if you spell them out spell *fuck.*"

Bikel is rightfully hailed as one of the most important and most dedicated advocates of twentieth-century Jewish music. Though born in Vienna, he spent most of his career hopscotching national borders in the name of the arts—a teenager in Palestine, a theater student in London, a founder of the Newport Folk Festival during his heyday in Greenwich Village, and a delegate to the 1968 Democratic convention in Chicago. But talk to him about his album covers and he's quick to admit to how much artifice went into constructing their visions of musical purity. Take *Theodore Bikel Sings Songs of Israel*. "This is not Israel," he says of the bucolic farm plot on the cover. "This is Long Island. Everyone wrote letters wanting

Theodore Bikel
Theodore Bikel Sings More Jewish Folk Songs
Elektra, 1959

Theodore Bikel
Songs of Russia Old & New
Electra, 1960

Theodore Bikel
Songs of a Russian Gypsy
Elektra, 1958

to meet this *halutz* girl from the kibbutz, this girl who pioneered the land of Israel and made it bloom. This girl was a model who they got in New York and took her to Long Island, into a field, gave her a hoe, and shot the picture. It looked as authentic as could be. It's the only phony thing on this record."

Bikel's LP cover designers worked hard to frame him as an industrious song cosmopolitan. He posed with Geula Gill ("She now has a smaller nose than this") amid piles of international-stamped suitcases and trunks on their 1959 *Folk Songs from Just About Everywhere.* He sat atop Elektra Records founder Jac Holzman's private plane for 1963's *On Tour* ("This was Teterboro, New Jersey") and time-traveled across Russian history on 1960's *Songs of Russia Old and New* ("That's me as old Russia and new Russia, all summed up in a change of a hat").

He had already "visited" Russia on 1958's *Songs of a Russian Gypsy,* only the cover was shot in a Manhattan photo studio. "The shirt I am wearing here was made by my mother when I was still in Palestine," he says. "The art director thought we needed a woman on the cover, so that's why she's there. She is definitely not gypsy."

Bikel's earnest polyglot folk style struck a serious chord with record buyers in the sixties. He went on to release an impressive sixteen LPs for Elektra, even outselling blues and folk legends like Oscar Brand and Josh White. "I made a lot of money for the company because it wasn't just Jews who were buying these records," says Bikel. "The big office that Elektra moved into had a subtitle—the House That Theo Built."

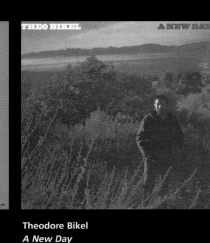

Theodore Bikel
From Bondage to Freedom
Elektra, 1961

Theodore Bikel
On Tour
Elektra, 1963

Theodore Bikel
A New Day
Reprise, 1969

CONCLUSION

Once the 1980s arrived with a flurry of drum machines and fluorescent socks, the needle was beginning to fall off the record. The advent of the compact disc and the dawn of the digital era turned LPs into antiques almost overnight. Outrun by technology, the once proud LP became mortal, twelve inches of scratched vinyl and flaking cardboard that was ushered out of the living room and into the thrift store, or left on the front lawn to warp in the sun during a weekend yard sale.

The music industry knew there was money to be made by granting some LPs a second life on CD, reissuing and remastering them to squeeze a dollar from fans old and new. But that was a tiny, lucky minority. The bulk of LP releases didn't make the cut and were left to live out their years in their original forms, risking extinction with each move. This book is full of the ones that didn't make it to CD, LPs that stayed LPs and, as a result, drifted swiftly to the invisible margins of history.

The possibility that these endangered audio species might actually be lost forever and that entire chapters of American and Jewish life would be forgotten because of a change in format only firmed up the importance of our journey to create this book. We had stared at those two photographs of our distant relatives long enough to know just how painful and frustrating lost histories can be. In putting this book together, we were able to put our own stories together and better understand our relationship to the Polish butchers and Hungarian soldiers who, like all these LPs, had become orphaned by progress. Thanks to these album covers, the distance between our lives and the lives contained in those old family photographs is no longer such a void. Now it's a landscape populated by characters as risqué as Belle Barth, as flamboyantly holy as Sol Zim, as worldly and socially committed as Theodore Bikel, as elegantly Yiddish as the Barry Sisters, and as steadfast and dedicated as Gadi Elon.

When we began this journey, we were inspired by the story of Abraham Zevi Idelsohn, the godfather of Jewish musicology who penned the lyrics to "Hava Nagila" and changed it from an obscure Hasidic tune into a must-play-at-every-wedding-and-bar-mitzvah pop song that everyone from Cuban salsa queen Celia Cruz and Lebanese guitar god Dick Dale have taken a swing at. Idelsohn spent the first half of the twentieth century gathering Jewish songs and eventually compiled the ten-volume *Thesaurus of Hebrew Oriental Melodies*. He was a Latvian Alan Lomax—only Idelsohn wasn't after preserving Appalachian folk tunes or African-American prison laments on a reel-to-reel deck. Idelsohn was after music that was supposedly his own—a Jew looking for Jewish songs in order to know what Jewish music was, to help define and preserve the legacy of his people. He knew that the definition of Jewish music, not to mention the definition of Jewish itself, was forever in process; the music was just as important as the act of gathering it, the act of seeking out what others had not found or had chosen to forget. Idelsohn's *Thesaurus* is typically remembered as a definitive, one-stop home, an authoritative source for all things relating to Jewish music. But it's also a testament to the scattered and the recuperated, to the personal tastes and quirks that are handed down as history.

We are no Idelsohns, that's for sure, and this has never been intended to be a *Thesaurus* of anything. But we'd like to think that we do share a mission: to gather music in order to find out who "we" are—as individuals, as a people, as a culture based in discontinuity. In collecting these LPs, we hope to contribute to Idelsohn's project by continuing to gather up the pieces of Jewish life. If collecting songs helped Idelsohn understand Jewish music, and by extension "Jewish" itself, then what happens when a collection emerges from a whole different stockpile? What new definitions await us?

Our journey is not over. Our goal is to raise the resources to win the race against time and track down the rest of the musicians we have found and record their stories before they pass on and their histories die with them. As Aaron Lansky, the founder of the National Yiddish Book Center and another one of our heroes, once wrote of his own quest to save Yiddish books, we too aim to "outwit history." If you are sitting on any musical treasures of your own (or are a musical treasure yourself!) we would love to hear from you. Please be in touch with us via our website and let the new histories begin.

by Dana Ferine

A F T E R W O R D

By Maira Kalman

I was born in Tel Aviv in 1949. One year after the state of Israel was established. My parents had come from small villages on the border of Russia and Poland. What did they know about music? Songs sung in the synagogue, klezmer musicians coming to the village for weddings.

In Tel Aviv there were tango orchestras playing in seaside cafés. Poets and musicians were coming from all over the world and they started to write songs about their new land. And about lost lands.

In 1954 we moved to New York. My father was a diamond dealer and he had business on Forty-seventh Street. We lived in the Bronx— mostly Jewish families who believed in culture. We did not buy books. We went to the library and started at A and continued in great happiness through the alphabet.

And even though I had piano lessons, my parents were not really interested in music. We had a radio and my sister and I listened to American standards and rock and roll. Then one day a huge Grundig stereo set arrived. A big shiny brown thing on legs with a cover that hinged up and a gold Grundig logo on the front.

The extraordinary thing was not that a stereo system had arrived in the home of a musically ignorant family. It was that it was a German product and my father, who lost most of his family in the Holocaust, forbade German products to taint our lives. I never asked why the change. But it was a miraculous one.

Records started appearing in the house. A weird mishmash of stuff. There was nothing better than playing the records over a million times and memorizing all the words. Friends would come over. We would just spend the afternoon singing. And the music was often great for dancing. It was a complete musical theater in the living room.

Barbra Streisand's *My Name Is Barbra* came as a birthday present, along with *Fiddler on the Roof* and the Dodaim singing Hebrew folk songs. The music was full of sadness and optimism at the same time. We were not at all religious Jews. We were Nova-on-Sunday-for-brunch Jews. But we were also Israelis and very proud of that. We were vitally connected, and this archive of music was one of the ways that we maintained the connection.

The records were stacked in the Grundig cabinet and often were strewn all over the floor. The covers were explosions of color and extraordinary energy. Seductive, funny, fabulous fashion. All of it was a fizzy cocktail of showbiz glamour and pride of origin.

We were the modern glamorous Jews.

And then a few years passed and they started to look embarrassing. Schlocky, not chic. Then we were getting older and interested in new things. Theodore Bikel out, Beatles in.

Bob Dylan, Bach, and Beethoven dealt the final blows to my old collection.

Now I look at these covers and some of them are so ridiculous and even more embarrassing than I remember. But I would like to think about the best of them and the shiny rectangular packages that gave so much pleasure. The mingling of cultures and great names in music and just music itself, which is the greatest thing there is.

And even still my sister and I can readily sing our favorite part of our favorite Theodore Bikel song:

In the corner is standing Natasha,
all the men are beginning to pant.
When she's dancing her shoulders they vibrate,
and when she's singing you see
that she can't.

Maria Kalman

CONTRIBUTOR BIOS

Wil-Dog Abers is a bass player and producer best known for being a member of Ozomatli, the Grammy Award–winning, politically charged Los Angeles Latin funk hip-hop band. In 2007, Ozomatli traveled through the Middle East and South Asia as cultural Ambassadors sponsored by the U.S. State Department.

Shalom Auslander is the author of the critically acclaimed books *Beware of God* and *Foreskin's Lament*. He has written for *the New Yorker, GQ, Time,* the *New York Times,* and the *New York Times Magazine.* He lives somewhere, with some others and some pets.

Aimee Bender is an acclaimed novelist and short story writer. She is the author of *The Girl in the Flammable Skirt, An Invisible Sign of My Own,* and *Willful Creatures,* and her fiction has appeared in the *Paris Review, McSweeney's, Tin House,* and *Granta.* She is a professor of English at the University of Southern California.

Sandra Bernhard is a comedian, actress, author, and singer who believes that to be the chosen people it is our obligation to reach out and share our wisdom and love with everyone, to look beyond our own horizon and include all mankind.

Lamont Dozier is the legendary Grammy Award–winning Motown songwriter who as part of the Holland-Dozier-Holland song-writing and production team was responsible for some of the most beloved hits by the Supremes, Martha and the Vandellas, and the Four Tops. Now a solo artist and producer, his songs have been covered by everyone from the Beatles and the Rolling Stones to James Taylor and Mariah Carey.

Etgar Keret is one of the leading voices in Israeli literature and cinema. His books have been published in twenty-five languages. The movie *Jellyfish,* directed by Keret and his wife, Shira Geffen, won the prestigious Camera d'Or prize at the 2007 Cannes Film Festival. His latest story collection, *The Girl on the Fridge,* was published in the United States by Farrar, Straus, and Giroux in April 2008.

Norman Lear is the Emmy Award–winning television writer and producer behind classic shows such as *All in the Family, Sanford and*

Son, The Jeffersons, Good Times, and *Maude.* He is also a visionary activist, founding People for the American Way in 1981 and most recently Declare Yourself, a nonpartisan campaign to empower eighteen-year-olds in America to register and vote.

Ann Powers is the chief pop-music critic for the *Los Angeles Times.* The former music editor of the *Village Voice* and pop critic for the *New York Times,* she is the author of *Weird Like Us: My Bohemian America,* and, with Tori Amos, *Tori Amos: Piece by Piece.*

Josh Rosenfeld is cofounder and president of Seattle indie label Barsuk Records, ancestral home of many of the finest and most intriguing musicians and songwriters of recent years, including Death Cab for Cutie, Nada Surf, Menomena, Mates of State, the Long Winters, Jesse Sykes & the Sweet Hereafter, Rocky Votolato, Rilo Kiley, and more.

Oliver Wang is a professor of sociology at California State University–Long Beach and a regular contributor to NPR, *Vibe,* and *Wax Poetics.* He runs the renowned audioblog www.soul-sides.com.

Michael Wex is a novelist, playwright, lecturer, performer, and author of books on language and literature. His books include *Born to Kvetch, Just Say Nu, Shlepping the EXILE,* and *The Adventures of Micah Mushmelon, Boy Talmudist.*

BIBLIOGRAPHY

In writing this book, we relied on a number of texts for historical reference, social context, and biographical information. . . .

Joey Adams and Henry Tobias, *The Borscht Belt* (Bentley, 1959)

Phil Baines, *Penguin by Design: A Cover Story 1935–2005* (Penguin, 2005)

David Ben-Gurion, *David Ben-Gurion in His Own Words* (Popular Library, 1968)

David Biale, *Cultures of the Jews: A New History* (Schocken, 2002)

David Biale et al (eds.), *Insider/Outsider: American Jews and Multiculturalism* (UC Press, 1998)

Theodore Bikel, *Theo* (HarperCollins, 1994)

Eugene M. Borowitz, *The Mask Jews Wear: The Self-Deceptions of American Jewry* (Simon & Schuster, 1973)

Joseph Boskin, *Rebellious Laughter: People's Humor in American Culture* (Syracuse, 1997)

Phil Brown, *In the Catskills: A Century of Jewish Experience in "The Mountains"* (Columbia UP, 2004)

Hasia Diner, *In the Almost Promised Land: American Jews and Blacks 1915–1935* (Johns Hopkins, 1977)

Arnold M. Eisen, *The Chosen People in America* (Indiana, 1995)

Ken Emerson, *Always Magic in the Air: The Bomp and Brilliance of the Brill Building Era* (Viking, 2005)

Lawrence J. Epstein, *The Haunted Smile: The Story of Jewish Comedians in America* (Public Affairs, 2001)

Leonard Fein, *Where Are We?: The Inner Life of*
America's Jews (HarperCollins, 1989)

Sylvia Barack Fishman, *Jewish Life and American Culture* (SUNY UP, 2000)

Myrna Katz Frommer and Harvey Frommer, *It Happened in the Catskills* (Harvest, 1991)

Leo Fuld, *Refugee: The King of Yiddish Music* (self-published, 1970)

J. J. Goldberg, *Jewish Power: Inside the American Jewish Establishment* (Basic Books, 1997)

Samuel Heilman, *Portrait of American Jews: The Last Half of the Twentieth Century* (Washington UP, 1995)

Will Herberg, *Protestant–Catholic–Jew: An Essay in American Religious Sociology* (Chicago UP, 1983)

Arthur Hertzberg, *The Zionist Idea: A Historical Analysis and Reader* (JPSA, 1997)

J. Hoberman and Jeffrey Sandler, *Entertaining America: Jews, Movies, and Broadcasting* (Princeton, 2003)

Abraham Z. Idelsohn, *Jewish Music: Its Historical Development* (Dover, 1992)

Samuel S. Janus, "The Great Jewish-American Comedians' Identity Crisis" (*American Journal of Psychoanalysis*, 1980)

Samuel S. Janus, "The Great Comedians: Personality and Other Factors" (*American Journal of Psychoanalysis*, 1975)

Jenna Weissman Joselit, *The Wonders of America* (Hill and Wang, 1994)

Mickey Katz, *Papa, Play for Me* (Wesleyan UP, 2002)

RB Kitaj, *First Diasporist Manifesto* (Thames & Hudson, 1999)

Aaron Lansky, *Outwitting History* (Algonquin, 2004)

Charles Liebman and Steven M. Cohen, *Two Worlds of Judaism: The Israeli & American Experiences* (Yale UP, 1990)

John Limon, *Stand-up Comedy in Theory, or, Abjection in America* (Duke UP, 2000)

Jennifer McKnight-Trontz and Alex Steinweiss, *For The Record: The Life and Work of Alex Steinweiss* (Princeton Architectural Press, 2000)

Jeffrey Paul Melnick, *The Right to Sing the Blues: African-Americans, Jews, and American Popular Song* (Harvard UP, 2001)

Andre Millard, *America on Record* (Cambridge, 1995)

Deborah Dash Moore, *To the Golden Cities: Pursuing the American Jewish Dream in Miami and L.A.* (Harvard UP, 1996)

Peter Novick, *Holocaust in American Life* (Mariner, 2000)

Michael B. Oren, *Six Days of War: June 1967 and the Making of the Modern Middle East* (Presidio Press, 2003)

Randall Riese, *Her Name Is Barbra* (Birch Lane, 1993)

Esther Romeyn and Jack Kugelmass, *Let There Be Laughter!: Jewish Humor in America* (Spertus, 1997)

Samuel Rosenblatt, *Yossele Rosenblatt: The Story of His Life as Told by His Son* (FSG, 1954)

Philip Roth, *Operation Shylock* (Vintage, 1994)

Jody Rosen, *White Christmas: The Story of an American Song* (Scribner, 2002)

Howard M. Sachar, *A History of the Jews in America* (Viking, 1992)

Jonathan D. Sarna, "A Great Awakening: The Transformation That Shaped Twentieth Century American Judaism and Its Implications for Today" (CIJE essay series, 1995)

Jonathan D. Sarna, *American Judaism* (Yale UP, 2004)

Gershom Scholem, *The Messianic Idea in Judaism* (Shocken, 1971)

Mark Schwartz, "Players Club: Memories from the Days of the Mamboniks," *Guilt and Pleasure,* Issue 6, Fall 2007

Jeffrey Shandler, *Adventures in Yiddishland* (UC Press, 2006)

Avraham Shapira, *The Seventh Day: Soldiers' Talk about the Six Day War: Recorded and Edited by a Group of Young Kibbutz Members* (Scribner, 1970)

Artie Shaw, *The Trouble with Cinderella* (Da Capo, 1979)

Marshall Sklare, *Observing America's Jews* (Brandeis, 2006)

Eric J. Sundquist, *Strangers in the Land: Blacks, Jews, Post-Holocaust America* (Harvard UP, 2005)

Ethel Waters, *To Me It's Wonderful* (Harper & Row, 1972)

Wax Poetics Editors, *Wax Poetics Anthology* (Wax Poetics Books, 2007)

Dick Weisman, *Which Side Are You On?: An Inside History of the Folk Music Revival in America* (Continuum, 2006)

Jack Wertheimer, *A People Divided: Judaism in Contemporary America* (Brandeis, 1997)

Michael Wex, *Born To Kvetch* (St. Martin's, 2005)

Stephen J. Whitfield, *American Space Jewish Time* (North Castle, 1988)

Stephen J. Whitfield, *In Search of American Jewish Culture* (Brandeis UP, 1999)

Yosef Yerushalmi, *Zakhor: Jewish History and Jewish Memory* (Washington UP, 2005)

ACKNOWLEDGMENTS

Roger Bennett and Josh Kun wish to thank the following: The incredible Nat Tinanoff and the staff and volunteers at the Judaica Sound Archives of Florida Atlantic University, one of the hidden gems of the Jewish community, Lorin Sklamberg and Jesse Aaron Cohen of YIVO, and all of those who have mailed us disks over the past few years. We promise we will give them a loving home. Special thanks also to Neil Sedaka and Maira Kalman for their articulate support and all-around kindness.

All of the following have helped along the way in massive fashion: Ross Martin, Jody Rosen, National Treasure Eddy Portnoy, Mark Schwartz, Ari Kelman, Rachel Levin, Nathaniel Deutsch, Michael Cohen, Michael Arad, David Katznelson's parents, Bill Bragin, Mireille Silcoff and her mum, Jonathan Sarna, Aaron Bisman, Jack Wertheimer, Brian Huizingh, Miri Pomerantz and all at the Jewish Book Council, the remarkable Alana Newhouse and the Forward staff, and Michelle Jaslow for her web design on www.trailofourvinyl.com.

There are no finer designers than Marco and Anne Cibola of www.novestudio.com. Everyone should use them. Dana Ferine, who has nurtured this project with loving care from start to finish. We are indebted for her hard work, diligence, collage skills, and love of the Barry Sisters. Carrie Thornton has supported this project throughout, along with Erin LaCour, Jay Sones, Donna Passannante, Patty Berg, Shawn Nicholls, Rachelle Mandik, Gary Stimeling, and all at Crown. Our superagent Kate Lee has provided the support and sharp insight that we cherish.

This project would be nothing without the men and women who made the music in the first place. In particular, we are grateful to Irving Fields, Gershon Kingsley, Theodore Bikel, Dinah Claire, Topol, Fred Katz, Will Holt, Jon Yune, Ron Eliran, Bill Dana, Gadi Elon, and Sol Zim for picking up their phones and inviting us into their living rooms. If any readers know of any of the musicians featured in this book we would LOVE to interview them too. We are indebted to the entire Reboot network and its board for their encouragement. This book comes directly out of our work with the 5olc3 Reboot Stereophonic record label (www.rebootstereophonic.com), which aimed to do for Jewish sounds what Smithsonian Folkways has achieved for American music. Our collaborators in this endeavor are the amazing David Katznelson and Courtney Holt. None of this would have been possible without their unending inspiration, vision, enthusiasm, and hard, hard work. They are two of the most remarkable colleagues and friends that anyone could ask for.

Roger Bennett would like to thank first and foremost, the people of the Russian town of Verchofka Podoslk for expelling my great-grandparents in 1879. The staff and sellers on eBay for turning my insomnia into an opportunity to track down that rare Zim Brothers disk. The board and staff of ACBP, Charles Bronfman, the late Andy Bronfman, Jeffrey Solomon for challenging and encouraging me in equal measure. Dana Ferine for her thoughtful, creative and patient support throughout. Cabot Marks, Birdman Records, Michael Cohen at Deaf, Dumb, and Blind, Penny Lane Records in Liverpool, A Flock of Seagulls, Echo and the Bunnymen, China Crisis, OMD, David Hirshey, and all at ESPN Books. David Moyes, Joleon Lescott, and Anthony Bloch at Everton FC. All the citizens of Boca Raton, our Fantasy Island. Mr. McNally, Peter Powell, David "Kid" Jensen, and John Peel. Dov Charney. Irving Fields and Gershon Kingsley for blowing our minds with their sounds. The Kroll Family and Celia Dollar—especially to Lynn for offering me the right place to write and to Jules and all at Ontrack Data Recovery for saving my hard drive when it crashed. The Kirsch Family, particularly Simmy and Eric for letting me loose with Aaron Kirsch's record collection. Jamie Glassman, who has the rest of his life to learn to love jazz. The entire Liverpool Jewish community, Lee Park Golf Club, and especially the staff at Stapely Hospital. My parents, Valerie and Ivor, for not disowning me when I was expelled from Hebrew school while my father was president, Nigel and Rebecca, Amy and Jonathan, and Holly (R.I.P.). I am fortunate to be a member of the Academy of the Recent Past (www.academyoftherecentpast.com) and am indebted to the organization's research fellows for their support. Josh Kun and Ceci Bastida for their friendship, shared passion, and rocking this. My late grandfather Samuel Polak, pur-veyor of quality meats, man of style, lover of all things American, especially wrestling, and an all-around mensch. My boys, Samson and Ber, and my wife, Vanessa, for her patience, understanding, humor, fondness for Hall & Oates, and love.

Josh Kun would like to thank my grandmother Joni Kamins for buying me my first LPs and cassettes, everyone who so generously shared their knowledge, tips, stories, and LPs, especially Josh Dolgin, Marisela Norte, Oscar Garza, Elijah Wald, Joyce Antler, Donald Weber, Larry Gross, David Meltzer, Lorin Sklamberg, Louise Steinman, Jonathan Freedman, Jonathan Boyarin, and Jessica Pallingston. Special thanks to Jon Yune, Eddie Barton, Gershon Kingsley, Theodore Bikel,

Irving Fields, and Fred Katz for the conversations and inspiration, Steven Rafferty for his supreme research skills and patience, Sharon Dynak and the Ucross Foundation for the space and the time, Mickey Katz for changing the way I listened, Ron Katz and the Katz family for all of their support of my work, my students and the faculty and staff of the Annenberg School of Communication and the Department of American Studies and Ethnicity at USC, Norman Lear, Marty Kaplan, Johanna Blakley, Leslie Wong, and Scott McGibbon of The Norman Lear Center, Music Man Murray for letting me into his vaults and telling the tales, Record Surplus, Amoeba Music, Out of the Closet, Saturn Records, eBay, the National Council of Jewish Women, Dusty Groove, Fairfax Avenue, the basement of the Judah L. Magnes Museum, the fine city of Boca Raton, all the secret swap meets, the Reboot Network for all the idea incubation, Ken Brecher and The Sundance Institute, Elsa and Bill Longhauser, Rebecca Rickman, Mike Rogin (wherever you are) for a legacy to live up to, Joshua Tree and the Sunny Rd. cabin for the bountiful quiet, Roger Bennett for the hustle, the generosity, the ceaseless ideas, and for being an incredible partner, Vanessa for marrying Roger, the whole Bastida-Martinez clan, my sister Heather, my parents for all their love and for indulging the collecting bug, and most of all to Ceci Bastida for shining the way she does.

The LPs featured in this book come from either our personal collections, the collections of friends and family, or the collections of the Judaica Sound Archives of Florida Atlantic University's Boca Raton campus. Started in 2002, the JSA is a major center for the collection, preservation, and study of Judaica sound recordings. Visit their website at www.fau.edu/jsa. The JSA gratefully accepts recordings (both secular and religious) for inclusion in its collection. For further information call Nathan Tinanoff, founder and director, at 561-297-2207.

Lea Deganith's *Songs of Israel*, The Messengers, *The IN Jewish Sound*, and *Yizkor: In Memory of the Six Million* are from the Archives of the YIVO Institute for Jewish Research, New York.

A note on LP dates: Finding accurate release dates for albums released in the 1950s and 1960s can often be a daunting task. Albums were very often not dated, and album catalogs—especially those of independent labels—are often unclear in their chronologies, if they are available at all. We have done our best to find original dates, but when we've been unsuccessful we have provided the most accurate time frames possible.

ABOUT THE AUTHORS

Roger Bennett is a board member of the Academy of the Recent Past (www.academyoftheresentpast.com) and the co-creator of the generational histories *Bar Mitzvah Disco* and *Camp Camp: Where Fantasy Island Meets Lord of the Flies.*

Josh Kun is associate professor in the Annenberg School for Communication and the Department of American Studies and Ethnicity at the University of Southern California. He is the author of *Audiotopia: Music, Race, and America* (UC Press) and a contributor to the *New York Times,* the *Los Angeles Times,* and many other publications.

Bennett and Kun are the creators of trailofourvinyl.com and cofounders with Courtney Holt and David Katznelson of Reboot Stereophonic, a nonprofit record label dedicated to rereleasing lost classics of the Jewish musical past. Visit www.rebootstereophonic.com.

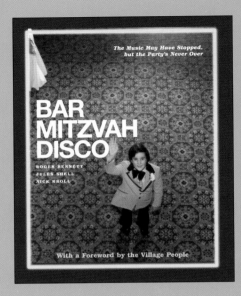

978-1-4000-8044-1
$23.95 (Canada: $33.95)

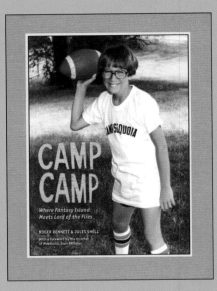

978-0-307-38262-7
$24.95 (Canada: $27.95)

Add to the Academy's Archives

The Academy of the Recent Past is dedicated to rummaging through the flotsam and jetsam of our lives. We are inspired by tales of the ordinary. Vinyl records, bar mitzvah photographs, and tall tales from camp are just the tip of the iceberg. Find out how to contribute to the Academy and be a part of our projects.

Available wherever books are sold.

ACADEMY
OF THE
RECENT PAST

www.academyoftherecentpast.com

Crown Publishers
New York
www.crownpublishing.com